Y0-AWH-713

‘NOTHING SO BECAME THEM…’

Some Improved Obituaries

MICHAEL GEARE
AND
DAVID HOLLOWAY

Illustrated by Tim Jaques

Nothing in his Life
Became him like the leaving it.
William Shakespeare, *Macbeth* I iv

BUCHAN & ENRIGHT, PUBLISHERS
LONDON

First published in 1986 by
Buchan & Enright, Publishers, Limited,
53 Fleet Street, London EC4Y 1BE

British Library Cataloguing in Publication Data

Geare, Michael
'Nothing so became them—': some improved obituaries.
1. English wit and humour
I. Title II. Holloway, David, 1924—
827'.914'08 PN6175

ISBN 0-907675-69-7

Typeset by Leaper & Gard Limited, Bristol
Printed in Great Britain by
Biddles Ltd, Guildford

CONTENTS

the principle of burnt cookery was one that he was determined to extend

POPULAR CATERING

(*incorporating* **Amateur Inn-Keeper**) **Yuletide 901**

King Alfred the Great

Among the many tributes that have been paid to the late King, perhaps his contribution to the art of cooking has been overlooked. It is surely the duty of this journal to set the record straight. It will be recalled that the King's first contact with the culinary art was unfortunate. But he never forgot the interesting experiment which he had unwittingly undertaken, and while burnt cakes may not have appealed, the principle of burnt cookery was one that he was determined to extend. Burnt toast was to find a considerable following, fish in burnt butter has proved an enduring success; and, in court circles, burnt lamb has proved popular as a sacrificial subject. Burnt sponge pudding was regarded as a failure, but surely his greatest triumph was his burnt custard. Indeed, so successful was this dish that, when introduced to it by His Late Majesty, the Carolingian King Odo ordered his cooks to follow the recipe. The Frankish *maîtres de cuisine* call it *Crème Brûlée*; in this country it will always be known as Alf's custard.

THE TIMES

1st April 1817

Vice-Admiral William Bligh

Vice-Admiral William Bligh died last week in London at the age of 63. Of yeoman Cornish stock, he enjoyed a distinguished naval career, serving with notable gallantry under Admiral Duncan at Camperdown, and with Admirals Hyde Parker and Nelson at Copenhagen.

Most astonishing in his career, however, was the fact that Admiral Bligh, an officer always noted for his wide humanitarian interests, was twice the subject of violent and malignant revolts against his kindly and ever-gentle authority. In 1808, when he was the Governor and Captain-General of New South Wales in the Australian colony (a colony still tainted with acts of wicked ingratitude and insubordination), this heroic officer was faced with a mutiny, from trumped-up causes, and actually sustained imprisonment for two years before returning to England and a well-deserved promotion to Rear-Admiral.

Even more extraordinary was his earlier experience in April of 1797, when his command, HMS *Bounty*, endured a mutiny on its return voyage from Tahiti, where bread-fruit plants were being collected for transplantation to the West Indies (Admiral Bligh's affectionate nickname 'Bread-fruit Bligh', stemmed both from his interest in the plant and the known amiability of his nature). The mutineers were led by an infamous ruffian ironically named Fletcher Christian (if he were indeed a Christian, he must have been of the

[*cont. on p. 11*]

Popish kind), and they cast their Master, and some loyal crew, adrift in an open boat to face inevitable death.

The Divine Hand of Providence, however, was here to be displayed. Most of the mutineers made their way to Pitcairn Island, where, happily, many died of disease or were massacred by the natives. Captain Bligh (as he then was) miraculously achieved landfall at Timor after a voyage of over 4,000 miles, and, returning to England, was appointed to command HMS *Providence.*

Often has it been said that such remarkable experiences, befalling so gallant and humane an officer (and one whose death is widely mourned throughout the civilised world and in the Australian colony), could have provided the basis for a realistic and moving theatrical production. Alas, it is now too late for this ever to be envisaged.

NEUE WISSENSCHAFTLICHE ZEITSCHRIFT FÜR KRIEGS-FORSCHUNG UND TIERKUNDE

October 1819

MARSHAL BLÜCHER

Field-Marshal Gebhard Leberecht von Blücher died last month on his Silesian estates. He was 77.

All the world knows of the Marshal's great victories over the perfidious French at Katzbach, Leipzig, Ligny and Waterloo — the last battle being his greatest triumph, although he generously accorded some credit to his subordinate, the Duke of Wellington. What is less known is that towards the end of his life, the Marshal was convinced that he was pregnant by an elephant.

It must first be recognised and accepted that in our present vastly developing world of New Science, the para-normal is now credible. The Marshal was a man of robust intelligence, and must have had solid grounds for his belief that he had been raped by an elephant: it may be scientifically regarded as an experience calculated to make a deep impression.

Two questions thence arise. The first — was the child ever delivered? — is more easily answered. The response must be 'No', for the existence of an elephant-child, or of a child facially resembling an elephant, would have been most widely remarked by physicians, savants and the extensive popular press throughout Prussia, England and France. It will be recalled that the Marshal, already, at 73, of an age when child-bearing could prove difficult, was knocked from his charger in a *mêlée* during the course of his victory at Ligny. And, although he seemed in his usual vigour two days later at

[*cont. on p. 14*]

scientifically regarded as an experience calculated to make a deep impression his great victory at Waterloo, it seems probable that the fall had induced an abortion.

The second question, on which the Marshal vouchsafed no clear information, is when did the coupling with the elephant take place?

Uncertainty as to the gestation period in this unusual instance — somewhere between the nine months for *homo sapiens* and the 22 months for *Elephas maximum* or *Loxodonta africana* — has not assisted our detailed enquiries into this aspect. It is certain that during the conceivable period Marshal Blücher was so totally occupied in military matters that he had no time or opportunity to visit a zöological park, nor even a circus.

Scientific reasoning thus suggests that the encounter must have been with an escaped creature.

We are therefore investigating possible escapes from circuses or zöological parks throughout the Continent with a zeal unabated by Marshal Blücher's untimely death, and remain confident that we shall yet be able to identify the putative elephant parent who so nearly broadened the horizons of scientific knowledge, and in so interesting a manner.

THE ERA

May 1865

John Wilkes Booth

Word has been received from Washington in America of the sudden death of John Wilkes Booth, a member of that country's first family of the theatre. He was 27.

There will always be controversy as to which member of this illustrious family was the finest performer. Certainly, Wilkes's brother, Edwin, has been the most successful, although many consider that he lacks the raw power of their late father, Junius Brutus. Wilkes himself, however, rose to the top of his profession very rapidly after he had abandoned his medical studies. He excelled in Shakespearian roles. Indeed, many would argue that his mode of acting was both more powerful and more spectacular than that of any other member of his family.

It will be remembered that he had perforce to cover his body with oysters to soothe bruises he sustained during the Battle of Bosworth whilst playing Richard III. There was, too, the occasion when his Desdemona stormed from the stage after suffering some injury when he flung Othello's scimitar across her 'dead' body. Perhaps his most original invention was to make his Hamlet, played, incidentally, in a heavy moustache, stark, raving mad from the moment the curtain rose until his death.

His final performance, and his most spectacular, was on 14th April of this year at Ford's Theatre, Washington, in *Our American Cousin.* The management

[*cont. on p. 16*]

caused some surprise by not including his name in the cast list, yet this may have been at the actor's request, since he spoke only one line, which he had himself added to the script of the play: '*Sic semper tyrannis*'. His subsequent and spectacular leap from one of the stage boxes is always likely to be remembered.

Unfortunately, for two reasons that performance of the play was never concluded. This was in part because Mr Booth sustained a broken ankle as a result of his magnificent leap and later vanished, in spite of his injury, and also because President Abraham Lincoln was shot. It is thought that the audience was enjoying the play, although Mrs Lincoln was not available to comment.

THE RECUSANT GAZETTE

April 1825

DR THOMAS BOWDLER

The death was reported earlier this year of Thomas Bowdler at the age of 71. For many — certainly for this journal — the greatest work in this most excellent man's life was his revision, his admirable *purging* of the plays of Mr Shakespeare. In Dr Bowdler's own words: ' . . . in my Family Shakespeare in 10 volumes; in which nothing is added to the original text; but those words and expressions are omitted *which cannot with propriety be read aloud in a family*' (our italics).

He set himself a noble task, and nobly he wrought it. But was it truly worth the wreaking?

It is our view that the works of William Shakespeare have been much overvalued. With their absurd coincidences, their gyronomonic circumbilivaginations and, above all, their content of vile bawdy, we find ourselves astounded that the plays have now survived the writer's death by more than two centuries. Indeed, numerous players, considered by many to be distinguished, Mr Garrick amongst them, have been pleased to perform these works, and even to be influenced by them; while it is said that their effect on the actress Mrs Sarah Siddons was such that she was unable to ask for the passage of salt or pepper at table save in pentameters.

Our preference is for nobler plays, *The Tragedy of Sophonisba* by the late James Thomson being a particular favourite. Nowhere in Shakespeare is there so

[*cont. on p. 18*]

powerful and arresting an opening line as: 'O Sophonisba, Sophonisba O'; perhaps the only comparable dramatic opening effect is in Mr Henry Carey's *Chrononhotonthologos*, where Rigdum-Funnidos enters crying — irresistibly powerfully — 'Ho there, Chrononhotonthologos, whither wentest Aldiborontiphoscofornio?'

No Shakespeare play achieves such grandeur, and it can be confidently said that the Tragedies, the *Hamlet*, *Othello* and *Macbeth*, are worthless. There may, however, be some merit in the Histories, and it could even prove that, as a consequence of Dr Bowdler's long, arduous and much-to-be commended labours, these plays will yet receive performances in future and less grossly permissive times.

Not every playwright will have the good fortune to have his words improved and purified by eminent scholars such as Dr Bowdler. What is truly needed is a Parliamentary Act specifying what speech may be uttered, what deeds and actions performed, on our theatrical stages. But this would be a great task, requiring the skill and wisdom of a Walpole, an Addington, a Pitt: none on the present Parliamentary scene seems capable of so noble an achievement.

THE SKYROS EFIMERIDA

25th April 1915

LIEUTENANT RUPERT BROOKE, ROYAL NAVAL DIVISION

We have learned, of course with regret, that an English officer, Lieutenant Rupert Brooke, recently died on our island and has been buried here.

We know little of Mr Brooke, save that he was a poet and apparently very keen on honey with his meals. He must have had a poor constitution, since our island paradise of Skyros, the island of Achilles, is universally known for its health-giving properties, and its marvellous ability to extend the life span of even the frailest humans, goats, poultry, etc.

But we cannot protest too strongly at learning that Mr Brooke regarded the ground in which he was to be buried as being, not Greek, but *English*. We find he actually wrote a poem in which he claimed that, should he be interred here, there would be: 'In that rich earth,' (he is right there, since our soil is unusually well-manured) 'a richer dust concealed/ A dust whom England bore, shaped, made aware ...'

Indeed, the verse opens with the absurd statement that, if he died on our beloved Skyros, then there would be 'some corner of a foreign field/ That is for ever England'.

This is as flagrant a territorial claim as was ever made by the bestial Turk on our fair land and islands. Our soil is sacred. Skyros is outraged, and

[*cont. on p. 21*]

'... some corner of a foreign field/That is for ever England': England must act to disavow its poet's insupportable claim our leading citizen, Eleftherios Haralambopoulos, is to undertake an eight-hour fast. The English Admiral, Jelliboe, should come to make an instant apology. England must Act to disavow its poet's insupportable claim.

MORNING POST

3rd January 1859

Mr Oliver Brownlow

Oliver Brownlow's life ended yesterday, a life in which early hardship was followed by the brightest of hopes, only to end in tragedy. His youthful days are widely known through the popular biography of him by Mr Charles Dickens, but the later events have not until now been recorded.

It will be recalled that, adopted as his son by the benevolent Mr Brownlow, he lived under that gentleman's roof for several years. On attaining his twenty-first birthday, however, young Mr Oliver Brownlow, able to claim for himself the £3,000 left from the wreck of his parents' fortunes, took courteous leave of the elder Mr Brownlow, and returned to his old haunts.

He indeed returned to the very area of Saffron Hill where he had endured so much and — although Fagin and Sikes, Nancy and the Artful Dodger were all dead — nevertheless gathered together many of his old criminal associates. Charlie Bates gleefully returned from his work as a Northampton grazier, Toby Crackit and Tom Chitling rejoined him, and so did Nancy's friend Bet. She was to become his common-law wife and bear him several children.

The only reason he ever vouchsafed for returning to the old quarters and way of life was: 'It was the first place where I ever had hot sausages.'

His gang not only carried on and extended the thieving and pick-pocket activities of Fagin's day; they

[*cont. on p. 23*]

also obtained large sums of what they termed 'protection money': unless shopkeepers paid them Danegeld, their stocks and shops would be destroyed. Curiously, he did not resume his earlier name of Oliver Twist but called himself Oliver Kray; the doors of shops which regularly paid their ransoms and were deemed safely under his 'protection' bore his initials 'O.K.', boldly marked in chalk. Such was his renown among his peers that these letters appear to have acquired some special significance in the vernacular of the underworld.

His reign as king of London's underworld finally ended last year, as a result of the indefatigable exertions of Inspector Bucket. Oliver Brownlow stood before the same wooden slab in the same court as Fagin had done twenty years earlier, and saw the judge don the same black cap. He was hanged in Newgate yesterday.

THE TIMES

27th July 1984

Mr William Bunter, CBE

William Bunter, the famous film director and producer, died last week at his home in Périgord, where he had lived since his retirement: 'I want', he said, 'to be closest to the very best truffles.'

Details of his age and his family background are scarce, although it is known that he was educated privately and at Greyfriars School. In fact, many details of Mr Bunter's schooldays were given in a weekly educational journal which flourished for many years, *The Magnet* (a publication which indeed was to provide one of the main intellectual drives of the NUT).

Leaving school, and eschewing university, Bunter quickly made his way in the film world, despite his phenomenal stoutness — 'I'm twice as fat as Hitchcock, but I'm twice as good a director', he used to say. His first major box-office success, and the first in a series of films in the same light vein and featuring many of the same players, was *Yarooh!* This was followed by nearly twenty motion-pictures, of which *Jack's the Boy*, *Harry's the Boy*, *Frank's the Boy*, *John's the Boy* and *The Bounder's the Boy* are best remembered. In a different genre, although equally successful, was his *Hurree Ramset Jam Singh's the Boy*, a subtle exercise in race relations in which the lead was eventually played by an unknown after Paul Robeson and Harry Belafonte had declined it. *Squelch* was less successful, although this delicate study of a tormented teacher is

[*cont. on p. 25*]

known to have influenced Terence Rattigan in his writing of *The Browning Version.* Mr Bunter was appointed a Commander of the Order of the British Empire for services to the film — or possibly food — industry.

Bunter never married, but remained very close to his sister Bessie, who died last year. Despite her brother's wealth and generosity, she had chosen to remain as a food-taster in a cake and confectionery manufacturing chain, the rapid growth and success of which are largely due to Mr Bunter's munificent patronage. He is, indeed, greatly mourned by many manufacturers and purveyors of delicacies.

JAMESTOWN JOURNAL

1st January 1822

Mr Napoleon Buonaparte

We should have noticed the death of our distinguished resident, Mr Buonaparte, on 5th May last year, in our last issue. But, as our readers know, because of the indisposition of Mr Zeb Cobbleigh, St Helena's leading chandler and the moving spirit of our *Journal*, the last issue never came out.

So it is only now that we can bid farewell to our resident, now interred on Mr Richard Torbett's estate.

Mr Buonaparte, although foreign, seems to have been quite a famous man — although not, of course, as famous as our Governor, Sir Hudson Lowe. He certainly spent a great deal of money with our local tradesmen; indeed, our butcher, Mr Gurney, says the bills for the foreigners up at Longwood House were bigger even than Sir Hudson's at Plantation House.

Mr Buonaparte, despite his funny ways, was generally quite well liked, but there were a few problems. He had this habit of chucking people under the chin or pinching their cheeks, and when he did this to Chloe Cobbleigh (she being just 17 and starting to be aware of things) her father gave him a terrible telling off as to where, and on whom, he was putting his hands.

'You mustn't talk to the Emperor like that,' said one of his friends, a Mr Montholon. 'Emperor, is it?' riposted Zeb, who is a great one for butterflies. 'Any more touching my Chloe and he'll be a Purple Emperor, I tell you.'

[*cont. on p. 28*]

of course there was a terrible scene when he beat Mr Buonaparte in five moves

But Mr Buonaparte really had been some sort of king of France (where he had Frenchified his name to Bonaparte), and had won several battles, too, which led to some more trouble.

It seems they played a lot of chess at Longwood House and Mr Buonaparte, having been a general, expected to beat his friends, Mr Montholon and General Bertrand and the others. Well, he may have been good at battles, but he was not at chess, and they had a hard time of it making sure that he always won. Then his valet, Mr Marchand, had the idea of bringing Joe Brewer up to Longwood; Joe was a few pennies short in the head but he knew the moves at chess. Of course there was a terrible scene when he beat Mr Buonaparte in five moves.

His servants were not very popular; Mr Marchand was all right, but his cook Mr Cipriani made some truly outlandish dishes, and his particular servant, Ali, was not only foreign but black — a Marmalade or some such, we believe.

All in all, however, Mr Buonaparte was quite popular — after he stopped his pinching — and we sometimes saw his funny little figure, with a little old spyglass, walking towards Dry Gut Bay or Buttermilk Point. He died of some trouble in his belly — there were those who said he was poisoned, but we believe it must have been Mr Cipriani's messed-up cooking — and we quite miss him on our island.

GLASSBLOWERS TECHNICAL QUARTERLY

January 1937

DAME CLARA BUTT, DBE

Dame Clara Butt, the famous contralto and concert singer who died last year aged 63 gave our trade a lot of difficulty.

There is no doubt that some of her purest notes, of great clarity and strength, actually could and did shatter glass — a phenomenon we are more accustomed to encountering with the high notes of sopranos. Perhaps because of the drier and clearer atmosphere this extraordinary occurrence was particularly evident in Australia, where she frequently toured with her devoted husband Robert Kennerley Rumford, himself an excellent baritone and most helpful in our researches.

These researches clarified the problem, but brought us little nearer to a solution. Glassblower Fred Pilkington accompanied her 1909 tour, and testified that at a Sydney concert all the balloon brandy glasses in the stalls bar shattered during her rendition of the *Indian Love Lyrics.* Identical glasses were produced in a different lehr, employing new techniques in the annealing process, but they all shattered at a subsequent concert in Melbourne during Elgar's *Sea Pictures.* This particular song also shattered plate-glass windows and car windscreens in Melbourne, and all the convenience bottles in the old people's ward when she sang to cheer them up in Brisbane General Hospital.

Perhaps the most remarkable shattering was at a charity concert in Canberra. The Austrian ambassador

[*cont. on p. 30*]

Count van Hotzendef had, since an injury from a Serbian bomb, worn a glass eye which he believed to be undetectable. As Dame Clara was concluding *O Sole Mio* it split in two; he remained unaware that the two parts had slid from the socket, until several of his entourage fainted away.

Dame Clara, though always co-operative and gracious, resolutely refused to abandon the singing of some of her most famous and successful pieces, although these appeared to be the most destructive. Happily, she made an exception when, to help the Great War effort in 1916, it was arranged that she should sing in a Versailles Salon adjoining the Hall of Mirrors. She agreed to change her repertoire, our experts humidified the Hall, and thus was averted what could have been a grave rift between the wartime Allies.

THE CORSICAN CHRONICLE

September 1566

LIEUTENANT CASSIO

Corsica has lost one of its greatest figures in the death of Lieutenant Cassio (the name by which he liked to be remembered, for although he was, of course, to rise to the rank of general, the 'little lieutenant' he will always remain to his island friends). Cassio's was the true figure of the career soldier. Born in Florence, he learned his early soldiering under the tutelage of the eminent Professor Niccolò Machiavelli, before being transferred to the Venetian army. There he was involved in an incident that could well have wrecked the career of a less determined man. He was placed under the command of an officer who had earlier shown considerable skill in guerrilla operations, but who was clearly unfitted for high command. When posted to Cyprus, General Othello became involved in an unfortunate dispute over the fact that a quantity of strawberry ice-cream was missing. He was about to be relieved of his command by a staff officer, summoned by Lieutenant Cassio, when the general, in a moment of mental aberration, killed his wife and committed suicide himself. The official report placed the blame on the lack of moral fibre among those with Moorish origins, a view with which Lieutenant Cassio entirely agreed.

With his second-in-command, Ancient Iago (who had been cleared of his part in the affair by the official inquiry), Cassio saw service in the private armies of numerous Italian princes. Between them they perfected

[*cont. on p. 32*]

the strategy of the battle waged with the maximum noise and the minimum loss of life. It was after the two wise warriors had fought four major campaigns in which no one was actually killed, that they were summoned to explain their policies, which they were able to do with great assurance. Unfortunately, after a dinner hosted by Prince Cesare Borgia, both the Lieutenant and the Ancient suffered severe attacks of food-poisoning, and came here to convalesce. Lieutenant Cassio's first marriage, to Signorina Bianca, had ended in divorce, but on his arrival in this island he was fortunate enough to contract a very happy second marriage with an heiress. The terms of the marriage settlement included a clause that the Lieutenant should take the name of his bride's family, something which he was more than happy to do. Buonaparte is a proud name to bear here, as the eight sons born in the evening of Cassio's life will attest.

Among the many mourners who attended the funeral were the twin sons of the late Ancient Iago, affectionately known as the Corsican Brothers.

With tears in his eyes, the Mayor at Ajaccio addressed the mourners: 'So, farewell, little lieutenant! As the Last Post sounds over your grave, soldiers everywhere join in salute to an old comrade who fought the good fight.'

BENT'S BOOTS & SHOE MAKER

August 1722

JOHN CHURCHILL, KG,
FIRST DUKE OF MARLBOROUGH

With the sad death of His Grace this June past, at the age of 72, we should record and give thanks for the inestimable benefits bestowed upon our shoesmith's trade, so blessed by St Crispin, through one of the great Duke's actions.

Such benefits accrued because Her Grace the Duchess, the lady Sarah, made a comment after one of the Duke of Marlborough's returns from the battlefields in the Low Countries. It was either after his first great victory as Captain-General of our Army, with the Prince Eugene of Savoy, at Blenheim (when the Marshals Tallard and Marsin were overpowered), or after his subsequent defeat of Marshal Villars at Ramillies; whichever it may have been, it was in 1707 that Her Grace's remark became widely known beyond Court circles. That remark was: 'My Lord returned from the wars and pleasured me twice in his top-boots.'

In the following year sales of top-boots in this realm were quadrupled and — as Her Grace's comment was yet more widely bruited — grew greatly throughout the Continent of Europe. Large orders were received, first from the wives and mistresses of Marshals and Generals, then from the ornaments of the great Courts of the Continent, especially from France and Holland, Austria and Brandenburg. We received large demands also from an international organisation set up in The

[*cont. on p. 35*]

in the following year sales of top-boots in this realm were quadrupled

Hague under the title 'Aphrodisiacs Anonymous'.

Our trade followed this tide of success, improving the design of top-boots to suit both battlefield and boudoir, developing techniques to increase both the softness of our leather and the fine-ness of our buck-skin.

Judge of our surprise and pleasure, therefore, when there developed, particularly in Holland, an additional large demand for boots of an unusually hard and martial nature. On our enquiring of our Netherlands agent as to the cause of this, they replied with a verse (which we suspect may be subsequently stolen):

In matters of Congress the fault of the Dutch
Is loving too little and lusting too much.

A league of our craft formed a Company to meet this continuing, growing and curiously varying demand. It was titled Kinki Boots. And when, in 1712, the Tories took power from the Whigs and our great Duke ceased to be the leading soldier and statesman of this realm, he — for a fee both generous and deserved — agreed to become Consultant to the Company, and so continued to the sad hour of his recent death. We mourn his loss.

GRASMERE GAZETTE

October 1834

Mr Samuel Taylor Coleridge

John Smith writes:

Your last issue carried much of the death in July of Mr Coleridge, the great poet, and so often a visitor to our friends the Wordsworths in Grasmere and Ambleside. But a word should be said of his prowess as a walker.

I walked with him over many years and many miles. Striding over Langdale Pikes and Coniston Fells, Elterwater Quarries and Sour Milk Force, talking of much — but not of poetry, for I am a plain man.

He was always eager to go walking and I remember once — it must have been in 1797, there had been business in Bristol — I went to call on him in his Nether Stowey home: although he was busy writing when I arrived, and seemed somewhat distracted, he hastened to welcome and stride out with me. I was staying, I recall, at Porlock.

THE TIMES

29th October 1861

The Right Reverend William Collins, MA, 99th Bishop of Southwark

The Right Reverend William Collins, Bishop of Southwark until his retirement in 1859, died last Tuesday. His death occurred at his estate at Longbourn, to which he was so deeply attached and to which he had added so greatly since it reverted to him from the Bennet family.

He was for 20 years vicar of Hunsford in Kent and there earned golden opinions for his devotion as a parish priest, particularly from his patron, the Right Honourable Lady Catherine de Bourgh, the widow of Sir Lewis de Bourgh of Rosings Park. Happily, Sir Lewis' nephew was a member of the Whig administration of 1832 and, the diocese of Southwark falling vacant in that year, Mr Collins' unremitting pastoral work — he wrote many of his own sermons — received its deserved reward in preferment.

As a Bishop he proved an outstanding success, addressing himself largely to the necessities for richer vestments and to the importance of active church support for oppressed members of the landowning classes. He spoke often and at length in the House of Lords, attacking — in his own words — 'the pride and prejudice of new-fangled economical and political opinions'. Lord Melbourne himself once observed to him: 'It is indeed extraordinary that you Lords Bishop know as much of politics as of theology,' and Bishop Collins generously allowed this to be a truth universally

[*cont. on p. 38*]

acknowledged.

He met the misfortunes of his private life with a deep Christian fortitude, and indeed talked of them openly and often. As a young man he was cruelly rejected by a cousin, Miss Elizabeth Bennet: although the man she preferred, a Mr Darcy, later found himself heir to a viscountcy, the Bishop was wont to say — with no trace of bitterness — ‘But she is wed only to a Lord Temporal when she might have had a Lord Spiritual.’ Later he was espoused to Charlotte, daughter of Sir William Lucas of Meryton. That marriage appeared made in Heaven, but soon after the birth of his first child — named William for his father and grandfather — Charlotte Collins was persuaded into a disgraceful attachment by the perpetual curate of Hunsford (such was the vicar’s devotion to his duties that the curate had ample leisure for such wickedness) and she, abandoning her child, fled with her lover to Brussels. Officers returning from that city in the following year, after the Battle of Waterloo, told Mr Collins, to his extreme distress, that the guilty couple were actually happy there, and prosperously engaged in the teaching of English.

Bishop Collins never married again. His son, the heir to Longbourn, early joined a book publishing company established by a connection in Glasgow when he was a child. It is believed that his firm may have a substantial future in the world of publishing: this was a source of enduring comfort to his kind and worthy father, now gone to meet his merited heavenly deserts.

EUGENICAL QUARTERLY

June 1780

CAPTAIN JAMES COOK

Ours is a new science, and it is with surprise and regret that we have to write in reprehension of Captain Cook, news of whose violent death last year in the Hawaiian Islands has just reached these shores.

Nothing can detract from his skill and courage as a mariner, explorer and circumnavigator. Without the Captain's marvellous navigation of our warships up the River St Lawrence, General Wolfe might have failed to secure Canada with his great victory on the Plains of Abraham before Quebec.

Captain Cook's fault lay in discovering the Australian continent. The Dutch had indeed touched upon it over a century before, but had wisely ignored it. For terrible consequences may ensue from this discovery.

Already serious plans are afoot to ship our felons and convicts to a settlement on the eastern shores of the country. Students of our new science must study the terrible possibilities: criminal men — and women — gathered together in this settlement, seamed in wickedness, procreating children who, from their dreadful parenthood and surroundings, will grow up yet more evil and degenerate. Imagine this process of debasement continued over several generations — imagine even, that, at a far future date some monster of accumulated depravity should somehow escape from Australia and make his way back to our own shores!

May I give you a personal example. In my own

[*cont. on p. 41*]

some monster of accumulated depravity
should escape from Australia

parish four criminals were lately tried and convicted — their names I remember as James, Everage, Murdoch and Callil. They were of a desperate nature — Callil, I recall, actually sought to justify the barefaced theft of a fowl on the mere grounds that her children were starving — and their transportation is mooted. It is fearful even to contemplate what, generations on and suffering an inexorable eugenical debasement, the heirs of such creatures may resemble.

The prospect is hideous. And, despite his many achievements and virtues, it is upon the late Captain Cook that the burden of dreadful guilt must forever lie.

APOTHECARIES', BARBERS' AND CHIRURGEONS' JOURNAL

January 1548

SEÑOR HERNANDO CORTES

Señor Cortes, the celebrated Spanish leader who completed the conquest of New Spain, died last year near Seville at the age of 62. Our correspondent in that City, Juan Grijalva (well known to our readers as the Barber of Seville) writes to us as to the probable cause of the great man's decease.

Juan reports that one of the men with the hero when they reached the west coast of New Spain (in a fine phrase likely to be employed again, he recalls how they looked at each other with a wild surmise) noted that Sr Cortes was silent, had eagle eyes and was already, over two decades ago, stout. It seems likely that he was of a glandular tendency, and Juan suggests that early victims of this complaint — increasingly frequent in the European world with rising economic conditions — should abjure richer foods. Our practitioners should recommend to sufferers that, to avoid stout Cortes's fate, they should partake only lightly of lampreys, fartes of portingale, pigs petitoes, tripe noumbles, mortrewes, rastons, Bosworth jumbles, frumenty and similar tempting delights, concentrating rather on a regular ingestion of the galingale root.

BENT'S HATTER & MILLINER

May 1836

COLONEL DAVID CROCKETT

Our trade will learn with profoundest regret of the death, in the Alamo fort in early March, of Colonel David Crockett.

Davy Crockett, as he was so widely and affectionately known, had an adventurous early career as hunter and woodsman in the southern states of America, and fought against the bloodthirsty Creek Indians with General Andrew Jackson. He soon entered politics, first in the State Legislature; then for nearly a decade in Washington in the National House of Representatives.

Happily for our trade, he always suffered from poor circulation of his ear-lobes and during his early days of outdoor activity was compelled to devise most ingenious warm furry hats with ear-flaps at once practical and highly attractive. In addition to his legislative duties, he quickly established Crockett's Gents' and Ladies' Hats in Bun Street, Washington, which became a Mecca for milliners. His *creations* for both sexes from the fur of racoon, squirrel, badger, beaver and sloth soon achieved almost legendary success although, for some reason associated with curing problems, his bold experiments with skunk were never entirely fulfilled. He also abandoned the idea of using for ladies' hats the skin of the mink, because of the uniquely vicious nature of the creature. It is believed, too, that Mr Crockett had been in communication with the British War Office with a view to establishing a bear stud farm and supplying

[*cont. on p. 45*]

His creations for both sexes from the fur of racoon, squirrel, badger, beaver and sloth soon achieved almost legendary success

the headgear of His Majesty's Regiments of Guards.

His untimely death occurred in a skirmish between Mexicans and Americans — a part of the so-called Texan War of Independence — in which several others were killed, although details are still sketchy. But whilst the Alamo is unlikely to be remembered, David Crockett surely will, his name an enduring inspiration to the hatters and milliners of the civilised world.

UNIVERS

27th April 1882

CHARLES ROBERT DARWIN

Few tears, surely, will be shed for Charles Darwin — Monkey Darwin — the English naturalist who died last week.

Born in 1809, educated at Shrewsbury Grammar School and Christ's College in Cambridge University, it seemed that he would do little harm when, in 1831, he set off with the British vessel, HMS *Beagle*, on a hydrographic survey of South America.

The voyage itself took five years, and it was not until 1859 that its evil fruits ripened, with the publication of Darwin's *On the Origin of the Species by means of Natural Selection.*

His hypotheses tended to the destruction of the Faith, the diffusion of the filthy leprosy of materialism, the shutting out of God from the heart of man. It is not surprising that the author of this evil is an Englishman. Nor that such a man should marry his own cousin. For over half a century his countrymen have asserted that 'God is an Englishman' (it must be noted that some of the new Americans think Him a White Anglo-Saxon Protestant). Since these views have been universally rejected by men of civilised and educated belief throughout the world, Darwin retaliated by declaring: 'If God is not English, *then there is no God.*'

We say that the savant who invented and propagated a doctrine so dreadful is both a fool and a criminal.

[*cont. on p. 47*]

That is what we say about Monkey Darwin. Unbelievably, the English yesterday buried him — the arch-destroyer of the Christian faith — with full religious honours in their Westminster Abbey. The hypocrisy, the madness of it.

THE GUNTERSVILLE LAKE GAZETTE

9th July 1870

MR CHARLES DICKENS

The death last month of Mr Charles John Huffam Dickens is reported from London. He was, of course, a well-known writer, but no friend of this great nation.

In several of his writings he made animadversions on America and its way of life, especially in *American Notes* and *Martin Chuzzlewit* which included observations as insulting as they were misguided.

These slights can be totally ignored, for this Britisher's own books show how worthless and decadent he and his country now are. Its aristocrats, as shown by *Sir Leicester Dedlock* and the *Marchioness*, are contemptible; its politics, as *Mr Pickwick* found at Eatanswill, corrupt; its racial intolerance and anti-semitism as depicted through Fagin [contd p. 5; see also 'Ku-Klux-Klan Grows Apace'] malignant; its educational system, as portrayed in *Mr Squeers*' school, inferior to that in many American States including, we avow, our own Alabama. Mr Dickens also delineated, in his infamous *Martin Chuzzlewit*, a typical English nurse, *Mrs Gamp*: readers will notice how badly she contrasts with our own nurse here in Tuscaloosa, Mrs Montgomery Koch, an angel of mercy and the wife of our respected Mayor.

Mr Dickens' works may at present have a considerable reputation but, we aver, a century from now they will be universally forgotten while those of our own Alabamian cane-break bard and writer Stonewall Hunt

[*cont. on p. 49*]

will be remembered throughout the world. We end with one of Stonewall's finest quatrains:

Throughout the world each black-plum'd hearse
   Must needs contain a loser
His life full flawed and far the worse
   Unless born in Tuscaloosa.

THE AMHERST INDEPENDENT

18th May 1886

EMILY DICKINSON

We announce with much regret the death at the age of 55 of Miss Emily Dickinson. She came from one of Amherst's oldest families and will be remembered as the daughter of Edward Dickinson, town lawyer and treasurer of Amherst College.

Miss Emily, widely known in the town as 'The Woman in White' was noted for her shyness, indeed she has not often been glimpsed in Amherst for the last 25 years, though her brother and sister who shared the family home with her reported that she was well.

The older members of the community will remember her as a bright and cheerful girl when she attended the Mount Holyoke Seminary and the Institute here. She did not take up any career, though it is rumoured that she may have been writing poems of some kind.

Whether, in fact, she had any talent is unknown since only two of her poems were published, and without her consent. The late Mr Henry Wadsworth Longfellow is known to have thought them of little merit. No doubt Miss Emily's claim to be writing verse was part of her make-believe life. Unfortunately we shall never know. Still, everyone will regret the sad passing of one of the town's characters.

THE TIMES

4th August 1986

PROFESSOR SIR JAMES DIXON

Professor Sir James Dixon, Kt, FBA, FSA, F.R.Hist.S., Master of St Janet's College, Oxford, has died after a long illness. He was 56. In a long career devoted to historical studies and university administration, few have contributed more than 'Jim' Dixon. His ten-year stint as Master of St Janet's saw many reforms which by the sheer force of his personality he was able to carry through meetings of often reluctant fellows. It was he who took the College away from the currently fashionable co-educational system, and recruited men only, and it was he who insisted that subfusc should be worn throughout full term. His ruling that only beer might be served in Hall arose less from his insistence that all water was polluted than from a belief that a regular consumption of beer would lead to improved athleticism. It was his pride that his college should contain more Blues than any other. The fact that it appeared lowest in the Moberley table, he dismissed with one of the grimaces for which he was famous.

Dixon, a proud product of the grammar-school system, took up his first teaching appointment at one of the most respected of our provincial universities. There, under the tutelage of the late Professor Welch, he was to lay the foundations for a career of unparalleled distinction, his work at the Gore-Urquhart Foundation bringing him into contact with the best scholars of his generation. His seminal work, *The Economic Influence*

[*cont. on p. 53*]

no voice was heard shouting louder

of the Developments in Shipbuilding Techniques, 1450 to 1485, won wide acclaim and was regarded by the late Professor Fernand Braudel as the greatest work of its kind. To this, 'Jim' Dixon added a series of readable books: *Merrie England*, *Merrie England Revisited*, *Love in Merrie England*, *Sport and Pastimes of Merrie England*, and the wittily titled *All that I Have Not Said Before about Merrie England*. This considerable output did not prevent him from contributing his regular fortnightly column to the *Illustrated Metropolitan News*, which, with his characteristic modesty, he entitled 'Quotes on the Face of it'. This journalism was widely admired for its refusal to acknowledge recent developments in any of the arts. 'Jim' Dixon's interest in sport came late in his life but no voice was heard shouting louder at Iffley Road, and his chair was permanently placed beside the sightscreen at the Parks.

Few men have travelled as often to the United States as did Dixon; indeed, it was his proud claim that he had held more visiting professorships in that country than any of his contemporaries. It was sad that his involvement with overseas commitments prevented him from fulfilling his lecturing commitments as Gore-Urquhart Professor of Oral History; a number of young historians, however, ably stood in for him.

'Jim' Dixon's marriage to the late Christine Gore-Urquhart was one of the happiest in Oxford, although, to the regret of both, they were not blessed with children. Lady Dixon's work among fatherless children has long been known and she could often be seen walking in the college garden with six or seven young people. She was always proud to say, 'These are my children', and jokingly her friends would say how like her her charges had become. It was an ideal marriage and 'Jim's' friends were often heard to remark how lucky he was.

POLICE GAZETTE

November 1930

SIR ARTHUR CONAN DOYLE

Superintendent Bassett (the Hound of the Yard) writes:

I was of course sorry to read of Sir Arthur Conan Doyle's death aged 71. I had nothing against the gentleman; indeed — having been Police Heavyweight Champion in 1894 — I much enjoyed his boxing books. But when he created his amateur detective, Sherlock Holmes, he really did make a terrible lot of trouble for the Force.

I remember the first Sherlock Holmes stories coming out in 1891 when I was a probationary Police Constable. What with the books and the stories in the *Strand* magazine and William Gillette portraying Holmes on the stage, within a few years we began to be plagued by all kinds of terrible amateurs thinking they could solve crimes better than the police.

They included all sorts of extraordinary people: lords, parsons, professors, funny old ladies and even foreigners from the Continent. Worst of all were 'private eyes' — all right for seedy divorce cases but useless for serious crime.

The trouble is that, although Conan Doyle is dead, Sherlock Holmes is not. When, after a lapse of several years, the author produced another batch of Holmes stories there was another upsurge of this regrettable amateur sleuthing, and even now I live in dread that Sherlock Holmes motion pictures may soon be made,

[*cont. on p. 55*]

with disastrous results.

I venture to take some space in the *Gazette*'s columns to indicate just how disastrous: here are some examples from my own experiences at the Yard with these characters who think they can do our job better than we can.

When we were investigating the Penge Severed Head Mystery, our Assistant Commissioner, a very social man, allowed Lord George Wimp, the Duke of Montana's son, to be involved in the case. Lord George persuaded the AC that no crime had really been committed as the severed member was undoubtedly the spare head of a Two-Headed Man with Yeti-type feet from Upper Siam, and the case was dropped.

Although the police were originally called in when very large sums were found to be missing from Borchester Diocesan funds, the Diocesan Council insisted that the investigation be carried out by a parson who had achieved some reputation as an amateur detective. He concluded that it was merely a bookkeeping error and the Hon. Treasurer, a minor Canon, was unfrocked as a punishment — this despite the fact that the Dean had gone to live in Buenos Aires with a mezzo-soprano from the Cathedral choir.

There was a particularly horrible series of murders in Camden Town just after the War, and we had substantial evidence that they were the work of a Northern villain living in London known as the Beast of Bolsover. However, an elderly lady amateur sleuth, once the Chief Commissioner's governess, told him firmly that, from her comprehensive knowledge of all human evil derived from a lifetime of educating the children of the aristocracy, she was sure the murders were not committed by a human being but by a large ape. We were instructed to make no arrest; the case was dropped and the Monkey House at London Zoo alerted.

More recent, and more bloody, was the case of the Swansea Slaughters. We were convinced that Slasher

[*cont. on p. 56*]

Jenkins was guilty: he was on our records, and those in Brussels, as being addicted to drink and then very violent (he drank methylated spirit of wood alcohol). Close to all the Swansea corpses were terrible scrawls of poetry, sometimes in the victims' own blood. We were set to arrest Slasher, but at the time we had a very posh Chief Superintendent — he wrote poetry himself — and his old tutor, then an Oxford professor, told him that Slasher couldn't have written the poems as they represented significant approaches to structuralism in *vers libre* and were the work of a highly educated man — which Slasher wasn't. Three murders later we *did* arrest him (he was later hanged, which was a mercy as he was a right psychopath), and we found his room knee-deep in his collection — of poems from Christmas crackers.

I could give other examples, but these would involve officers still living. Sir Arthur certainly did much good, as a doctor and a writer — but he also accidentally caused a fearful lot of harm.

PORT-AU-PRINCE POST

22nd April 1971

PRESIDENT FRANÇOIS DUVALIER

It will be difficult for we Haitians, but now is the time to cease grieving over the death, on that dreadful day earlier this year, of our universally beloved President, François Duvalier: 'Papa Doc', as he was so affectionately known. For 14 years he was our President, our life force, semi-divine yet so deeply and lovingly human.

But now we must turn our thoughts to the marvellous blessing of his son, Jean-Claude Duvalier, his successor who was yesterday elected — with acclamation — as President for life. 'I will ensure the economic revolution,' he declares, and under his rule we Haitians can be sure of continued happiness and even greater prosperity, with peace and tranquillity assured by the kindly vigilance of the Tonton Macoute.

President Jean-Claude Duvalier is young. Tall, elegant, nobly proportioned, he yet has marvellous qualities of humility and self-denial. Many nations would welcome him to their shores as their ruler, but it is our blessed fortune that he will remain our loved leader, our beneficent master, for the rest of his life; if we are truly fortunate, this prospect of enduring happiness will continue well into the next century. How incomparable is the bliss of the Haitian people.

Charles Magloire, Editor.

PORT-AU-PRINCE POST

24th April 1971

Our late Editor Charles Magloire was executed today. He was most justly sentenced to immediate execution for the gross lack of respect shown to our adored President in using in his article of 22nd April, the word 'humility' in respect of our heroic leader.

GOLFING MONTHLY

April 1969

General Dwight D. Eisenhower

Dwight David Eisenhower, who died last week from a heart attack, aged 78, was internationally recognised for his services to golf. He spent most of his childhood in Abilene, Kansas, trying to play the game; subsequently finding the course at West Point incomparably better, he spent so much time there that he was 25 before he was commissioned into the US Army in 1915. Although anxious to go to the Western Front when the US later entered the war, he was deterred by reports of poor golfing facilities in France.

Between the wars he served in the Philippines, and on the Manila Municipal Course, where he set a record-playing round twice in a day for an aggregate of 407 strokes (par was 72). He had become an attacking player — his advance along a fairway was marked by divots on a broad front — with a particular fondness for using the cleek; to which he later wrote a brief encomium *I Like Cleek.*

By the outbreak of World War 2 Dwight, between handicap tournaments, had progressed to lieutenant-colonel; he was soon promoted and sent overseas and, although disappointed with Tunisian golf courses, found great fulfilment on those in Britain and France. His charming wife, Mamie, was now reconciled to being a Golf Widow. She took up the launching of ships and, although she had not exactly the face for it, must have launched at least a thousand.

[*cont. on p. 61*]

although disappointed with Tunisian golf courses, found great fulfilment on those in Britain and France

After the war he sometimes returned to England to fight old battles, at Sunningdale. In 1955 he thought he had sunk the largest putt of his career — 38 inches — when the ball inexplicably popped out of the hole again. He recovered completely from the ensuing heart attack, continuing with regular play his total dedication to his life's work.

Dwight was also 34th President of the USA.

MORNING POST

26th June 1881

SPURIOUS EARL SHOT DEAD

Cedric Errol, claimant to the Earldom of Dorincourt, has been shot dead by the Sheriff of Lincoln County, New Mexico, United States of America, after a gun battle, it was learned in London yesterday.

Errol (21) made headlines when he was brought to London by Hobbs, a New York grocer, pretending to be the rightful heir to the Dorincourt title. The conspirators, Hobbs, a boot-black and a woman calling herself 'Dearest' who claimed to be the boy's mother, persuaded the elderly and frail Earl of Dorincourt that the boy was his long-lost grandson. As a result Errol assumed the courtesy title of Lord Fauntleroy.

On the death of the Earl, Hobbs and the others presented Letters Patent to the College of Arms who were very quickly able to discover that the 'Lord Fauntleroy's' aspirations were entirely without foundation.

In order to avoid another Tichborne case, the Director of Public Prosecutions recommended the deportation of the persons concerned. However, the police prosecuted Hobbs for forgery and he was sentenced to six years' penal servitude.

On the voyage to the United States, Errol is said to have made the acquaintance of an English bachelor, John Tunstall; from then on, until Tunstall's murder five years later, the two were inseparable companions.

After a short and unhappy period in New York, the two set out for the frontier area of New Mexico, with Errol assuming the name of William Bonney. 'Dearest', it is thought, resumed her old (the oldest) profession.

[cont. on p. 63]

Tunstall and 'Bonney' established themselves in New Mexico where under the cover of cattle ranching they continued a career of crime. In due course, the elder man, Tunstall, was shot in a battle with a rival gang, starting the so-called Lincoln County War. Bonney set out to avenge his partner and over a period of months committed a number of murders. He was apprehended, but escaped from the gaol in Sante Fe.

Shortly after, he was cornered by Mr Pat Garrett, the local sheriff, and shot dead. When Mr Garrett was told that his victim claimed to be the Earl of Dorincourt, he said: 'Maybe he is some sort of limey Lord, but to me young Billy will be just a punk kid. And no one will remember his name in six months' time.'

CHIPPING TOAD CHRONICLE AND DISTRICT ADVERTISER

2nd November 1997

MR MICHAEL GEARE

Michael Geare, who was a Toad resident for many years, died last week. He was known in the district for his work on the Parish Council.

In 1986 the Vicar of St Mary the Virgin, Chipping Toad, the Revd Mr Pluckrose suggested that his eight choirboys be provided with handkerchiefs as, in winter months, they spent more time wiping their noses with the backs of their hands than singing.

The Parish Council devoted several meetings to this important issue. This paper reported them in detail, but can now write more freely as all the protagonists are deceased. Mrs Tickell, of Tickell & Hassock, the independent grocers, loudly maintained that the choirboys should stand on their own two feet and, unsubsidised, provide their own hankies.

Mr Jones, the upholsterer from Wales, a voluble man with acne, maintained that the church was old and draughty, indeed fifteenth-century, and should be torn down and replaced with a warm, dry, prefabricated building: this would obviate colds and give local employment. Dr Dearth — whose practice was small as many Toad residents preferred the advice of Mr Vyles the veterinary surgeon — spoke for some hours on the mistaken foreign policies of Bolivia, Ecuador and Upper Volta, where running noses were an endemic problem. Mr Geare then went to the summer sale of the Chipping Stoat Co-op's drapery and haberdashery

[*cont. on p. 65*]

department and bought 24 handkerchiefs. The choirboys used these for several weeks.

In addition to this, Mr Geare wrote several books. Some are in our local library, but our branch librarian, Miss Chickbane, tells us that nobody reads them.

He was married to the well-known travel writer, Carol Wright, but she was abroad at the time.

MANUSCRIPT NEWSLETTER IN ST COLUMBA'S MONASTERY, IONA

Winter 604

His Holiness Pope Gregory the Great

Tidings reach us from the South that Pope Gregory died in the summer. His Holiness — universally beloved since his election to the Papacy in September 590, following the death of Pope Pelagius II — needs no further praise from us for his wisdom, saintliness and many achievements, not least the sending of Augustine to these shores.

We would write only of three small blemishes on his great achievements which have led some to speak, however jestingly, of his papal fallibility.

His personal concern for the reform and standardising of the chant has made a few — we are not among their number — declare that too much spiritual time is now spent in chanting.

His quick and generous temper sometimes brought him to say to an importunate, 'Go — take a powder.' As a consequence, fraudulent physicians produced a great variety of Gregory's Powders; these were harmless enough when largely compounded of rhubarb and ginger (indeed beneficial to the bowels) but with other additives were sometimes fatal.

There were also doubts as to his misjudgement of British children, of whom he is reported to have said, 'They are not Angles but Angels.' But in truth His Holiness made no misjudgement here. His words were heard, and brought back to these lands, by British traders speaking only Isle of Dogs Latin. They misheard

[*cont. on p. 68*]

'They are not Angles, but Hell's Angels'

the Pope who actually, in his comprehensive wisdom of the true nature of British youth, said: 'They are not Angles but Hell's Angels.'

THE GUARDIAN

34th Mad 6891

ALF GRUNGE

Alfred Grunge, a stench trades onionist, and for many years before his retirement in 1982 the fothe rof the Chipple of *The Gadurain's* print shop, died yesterday in his Dagenham mansion. Dagenham mansion. He was. He was a well-known Dagenham figure as president of its golf club and owner of a local mini-cab fleet, and often appeared on Chanel No. 4 Television elequently explaining the hardships, in work and pay, of Fleet *Street compositors.2222—*

Tiny Dubbins, president of hi sunion, said, ‘me and all his NAG bothers see Alf's possing as a great lust: he was a fink man and a real fiend.’ The thieves were seen leaving thes cene ina white fOrd Cotina which was later fond abandoned in Mrs

MAINZ MESSENGER

May 1468

MEISTER JOHANN GUTENBERG

It is with the deepest grief that we write of the death earlier this year of Johann Gutenberg at the age of 71. A kind, good, sage man, he was personally known to many of us, and the printing of this very memorial is a tribute to his genius and invention.

And yet we cannot but wonder what History will write of his invention. Before it, reading and learning and knowledge resided with only a few men, wise and often devout, who played the greatest part in the ordering and governance of the affairs of countries.

But since his invention all may read, all may learn; humble men, huckstering men, ill-conditioned men — women even — and they could come to play much part in matters of politics and government. The Greeks of old had a word for so fearful a state of affairs: Democracy — government not by *Aristos*, but by *Demos.* It would be a dreadful thing if our good Gutenberg's invention should bring so great an evil as Democracy upon our civilised world.

since his invention, all may read, all may learn

LITTLE BIGHORN BUGLE

1st June 1986

DUKE JERZY GUTZ

Duke Gutz (49), whose soft-drinks manufacturing outfit, Gutz, Rott Inc., is one of the biggest employees of labor in our community, died tragically yesterday. He was killed when our recently retired sheriff, Earl Bollins, apparently overcome by a nervous collapse, threw a home-made petrol bomb at him as he left the Gutz, Rott lot.

The particular tragedy was that Duke had planned to leave the previous week on a month's visit to Europe. Though a man of rugged courage in the John Wayne mould, he had cancelled his vacation because of the epidemic of terrorism, bombings and killings now raging all over Europe.

Duke's grandfather came from Poland, and this part of Europe lies close to another part, Scotland. Duke last year discovered he had strong Scottish connections and, at the cost of several hundred dollars, bought membership of a clan, the Macmaxwells, and several items of Scottish clothing, tartans, kilts, pibrochs, sporrans, etc. He was heading for Scotland when the news that Colonel Gadaffi's Libyan terrorists were actively operating on their murderous work all over the Scottish Highlands made him call off the trip — with a result which has brought such grief to his family and our entire Little Bighorn community.

THE TIMES

5th January 1900

Sir Uriah Heep

Sir Uriah Heep, whose death from acute glanders at his home in Malling Manor in Kent at the age of 90 occurred on Tuesday, enjoyed a remarkable career with early misfortunes later replaced by richly deserved success.

He was born in 1810, of humble origins, near Whitstable where his father was a sexton. He qualified as a solicitor — he always claimed that he owed this to his unremitting youthful study of *Tidds Practice* — and became a partner in Wickfield & Heep, lawyers and stewards of estates, in Canterbury. This partnership was dissolved after an unfortunate dispute: its details were obscure, but it was provoked by a man whom Sir Uriah (whose benevolence sometimes outweighed his judgement) had wrongly trusted as his confidential clerk, a Wilkins Micawber who later fled to Australia. A yet more severe set-back occurred some years later when Sir Uriah, falsely implicated in a fraud on the Bank of England, actually spent some time incarcerated in a Middlesex prison (he used, laughingly, to recall that his number there was 27) until, after an Appeal lodged by his devoted mother, he was released without stain or blemish on his character.

He rapidly built up the legal firm of Heep & Runne, specialising in City work. He bought an estate in West Malling and, as a respected local landowner, was elected for Maidstone in the Liberal interest in the 1868

[*cont. on p. 74*]

election. He continued as Member for that constituency until Mr Gladstone — with whom he enjoyed some friendship, with a shared interest in ecclesiastical studies — ended his administration in 1885. In the House Sir Uriah specialised in financial and religious matters.

Sir Uriah was a devout evangelical churchman — the Hymns were indeed his favourite study — and he invariably read the Sunday lessons at his parish church; but only the second, New Testament, lessons, as he believed that in them especially resided true Devotion and Humbleness.

He was an unflagging worker for charity. In particular, he played a dominant role in the administration of two charities, Fallen Women at Home and Fallen Women Abroad, for which huge sums were raised. Sadly, shortly after his wise, guiding hand was removed on his retirement in 1890, both collapsed in grave financial difficulties.

Sir Uriah never married. It was known that when young he was deeply devoted to the daughter of his first partner, Mr Wickfield, and that she rejected him in favour of a briefly successful novelist, D.T. Copperfield (the marriage brought much unhappiness). He never encountered any other lady to match her charms or expunge her memory. The baronetcy therefore lapses, and it is believed that the bulk of the large fortune of this much-admired public figure is bequeathed to Liberal Party funds.

THE TIMES

2nd February 1999

Lord Helpass

Lord Helpass died yesterday after a short illness. He was 66.

Born and bred in Bristol, Bert Frederick Helpass was very much a Westcountryman. The National Union of Whelksters is predominantly a Westcountry union, and his long association with it began early. After working briefly as a whelkster he became a Union official, and in 1978 was elected NUW president, an office he held with distinction for ten years.

He was fiercely opposed to any form of Government interference in the whelking industry, other than the provision of subsidies to sustain it. He was proud of the strike record achieved by his courageous resistance to successive Governments: in his decade of presidential office his members were on strike for an aggregate of four years and five months. A sad corollary to his splendid determination was the halving of the Whelksters' membership.

He was created the first Baron Helpass of Worle as soon as Mr Kinnock's administration took office in 1988. He then resigned the post of President of the NUW, and became Government spokesman on economic matters in the House of Lords. His unconventional economic theories were not always welcomed by Their Lordships, but his successful attempt to have their attendance allowances quadrupled received their almost unanimous support.

[*cont. on p. 76*]

Lord Helpass was much loved, within the Trade Union and Labour movements — at their conferences he was their most admired and applauded speaker — and by many friends overseas, especially in the Russo-European Empire and Libya. When speaking in these countries he never hesitated from a courageous denunciation of the brutality and oppression existing in Britain.

His finest hour came only last September when, having been despatched by the new Labour premier, Mr Hatton, on an appeasement mission to his old friend Colonel Gadaffi, he returned from his mission triumphantly successful. Landing at Heathrow (in the first aeroplane from Libya to land in a West European country for 10 years), he was able to display a signed document which, he ringingly declared, 'guaranteed peace in our time'.

THE POKER PLAYER

November 1876

US Marshal James Butler Hickok

The sudden death of the well-known poker player, James Butler Hickok, in the Number Ten Saloon at Deadwood, South Dakota, has been reported. Mr Hickok was a regular attender at the green baize tables in many parts of the Frontier area. He was an exponent of both the Stud and the Draw game. His almost uncanny habit of turning up a 'joker' led to him being given the nickname 'Wild Bill'.

Poker players all over the world will be much exercised by the problem of his final hand. He began a game at 'Number Ten' at 3 p.m. and had been wagering for several hours with those accomplished members of the poker fraternity, Carl Mann, Cap'n Frank Massey and Charlie Rich. The pots were high and Wild Bill's play was hot.

In the final hand Bill was dealt a pair of aces, a pair of eights and a low spade. Cap'n Massey folded and the other two contestants had each drawn two cards. Should Hickok have discarded his spade in the hope of drawing to a full house? Mr Jack McCall's sudden intervention in the game, with a bang, you might say, means that we shall never know what Hickok intended to do.

The Poker Player offers a prize of $5 to the reader who supplies the best solution to this problem. In making your choice it must be remembered that Hickok was a ruthless player cooling a number of his opponents. Send your entries to our New York office.

Bill was dealt a pair of aces, a pair of eights, and a low spade

THE TIMES

2nd September 1879

Sir Rowland Hill

Mr Anthony Trollope writes:

I have been requested by the Editor of *The Times*, Mr Chenery, to write a short memoir of Sir Rowland Hill, the notice of whose death last week in Hampstead has already appeared in these columns. I knew him, of course, well, for it is only 12 years since that I resigned from the Post Office after 33 years of service; in my later days there, when I was a senior Surveyor, he was the Secretary of the Post Office. More, since although I had already written a large number of successful books, so long as I remained in the Service my first duty and care was to that Service, we therefore had many meetings and discussions in the great headquarters in St-Martins-le-Grand.

De mortuis nil nisi bonum is the accepted phrase, but I think it better to write with full honesty about Sir Rowland. He had, of course, some achievements to his name: he was helpful in the reorganisation of the postal system in Britain and the Colonies; and he contrived the adhering postage stamp and introduced penny postage. This last innovation is destined to continue in perpetuity.

But he was in truth a dry, cold, bloodless man — I can only describe his appearance as snake-like — and entirely unfit to manage other men. He even tried on one occasion to prevent me from taking a well-earned

[*cont. on p. 80*]

leave of absence, and might even have succeeded but for the intervention on my behalf, of the late Postmaster-General, Lord Elgin. His proposals for the unnecessary colonisation of South Australia and his interest in Mr Robert Owen's dangerous socialistic schemes do not do him any credit, either.

His writing, like his judgement, seemed always to be flawed — indeed his *Plans for the Government and Education of Boys* appears to me as one of the most tedious works ever penned.

Sir Rowland was for much of his earlier life a school teacher. It seems probable that, given the nature of his talents, he would have succeeded better had he continued in that occupation.

UNDERTAKERS' JOURNAL

27th May 2003

Mr David Holloway

David Holloway, the writer of obituaries, is reported to have died while hard at work on his life's ambition, the writing of his own obituary. He was of uncertain age.

Holloway came to obituary-writing young. His first effort (1940), a brilliant summation of the career of A.C. Tulloch, formerly of the Bengal Service Corps, was well received, though some remarked at its similarity to the one appearing in *The Times.*

After his early success, he moved on to other newspapers and scored some notable firsts. His 'Thomas Mann' (1955), written and dictated by him while he was in his bath, was a sensation, while his 'A.A. Milne', published the following year, was regarded as a fine work of imagination.

Some of his later publications were regarded as controversial. His 'Enid Blyton', a lengthy work, was condemned by one critic as 'obituary writing of the most vicious kind', while that of 'Patrick Hamilton' was declared a work of fiction in that the hero was married to the wrong woman.

Holloway was indefatigable in his task, and published numerous examples during most years from 1960 onwards. His 'Agatha Christie' was a best-seller, but his own favourites were two poetic works, 'Philip Larkin' and 'Robert Graves'.

The writer was occasionally consulted by others, and, while much of his best work was written after he

[*cont. on p. 82*]

had been woken up at night (see ‘Evelyn Waugh’ and ‘Lord David Cecil’), his attempt to complete ‘Ezra Pound’ was regarded as a major failure. Rung up by the *Washington Post* at 3 a.m., he began confidently: ‘One of the five great poets of the century?’ Who, he was asked, were the other four? ‘Yeats, Eliot, Auden,’ he answered, and then his voice trailed away. The work was never published.

Holloway, who was married with three children, was also an author and reviewer of books.

POPULAR FLYING

2002 (Minoan Calendar)

Flying Officer Icarus

The first reports that the tragic crash of Flying Officer Icarus was due to pilot error have been denied. Although it is admitted in Air Ministry circles that the flyer may have been exceeding the natural ceiling of his performance, it is thought that there were other contributory factors connected with the design of the wing structure. Lord Daedalus, the designer, refused to be quoted, but it is understood that the accident inspectors are endeavouring to reconstruct the broken wing and are particularly interested in the wax utilised. The Air Ministry has issued a statement to say that all men have been grounded until the findings of the official inquiry have been published.

Lord Daedalus, the designer, refused to be quoted

EQUUS ET CANIS VENATICUS

February 793 AUC

INCITATUS

All who love that noble friend of man, the horse, will be deeply saddened by the news that the Emperor Claudius Caesar has decided to put down Incitatus, known as 'Bootikins', one of the finest 16-hand bay stallions ever to jump a clear round at the Circus Maximus. There were those who thought that his saddle, wrought of ivory and pearls, was somewhat ostentatious. But then, that fine owner, to whom the Olympic Jumping Team will always be grateful, the late Emperor (and God) Gaius Caesar Caligula, was always concerned that his mounts should have the best. Perhaps, too, there were some who thought that the late Emperor's training methods for riders in his team were a little over-rigorous. Even those whose speciality was the puissance did not relish practice leaps from the Tarpian Rock, although a visiting Briton, a chap called Bunnus Hicksteadus, promised his friend Caractacus (no mean driver four-in-hand himself) that he would, on his return home, set up a similar jump in his back garden.

The late Emperor's affection for his splendid mount is reflected in the fact that he gave to it his own nickname. It is only sad that circumstances prevented Bootikins from undertaking the duties that his master had so properly appointed him to. Every right-thinking Roman would have been happy to serve under so noble a consul, and to have worshipped with so devout a priest.

THE JERUSALEM HERALD

Easter 33 AD

JUDAS ISCARIOT

The Chief Priest writes:

I am sure that I am not the only friend of Judas Iscariot to be disturbed by the harsh tone of your short obituary published yesterday. To many of us, Judas was recognised as a man who knew where his duty lay and would let nothing prevent him from carrying it out. True, some people thought that he was a little over-demonstrative at times. His habit of embracing other men in public was a little otiose. Even so, when the full facts are known, his name will be remembered longer than those of many of his contemporaries in both the fields of internal security and horticulture.

Letter to the Editor

From the Governor of Jerusalem.

Sir,
Further to your obituary of Judas Iscariot and of the letter from the Chief Priest, I should like to make it clear that I washed my hands of the whole affair.
Yours etc.
P. Pilate,
Governor

CALCUTTA STATESMAN

23rd September 1972

Mr Sambo Jumbo

Word has been received from the Jungle of the sudden death of Sambo Jumbo, the 35-year-old leader of the Black Tiger organisation. It is understood that he was ambushed by a rival gang known as the Children's Librarians.

His mother said that Mr Jumbo, affectionately known to all as 'Little Black Sambo', had been a good son to her, his only fault being an over-indulgence in pancakes. However, as he grew to manhood, he had been constantly under pressure from those who wished to exile him from the Jungle. They accused him of sexism, racism, greed, exhibitionism, all of which he vehemently denied.

Eventually, sickened by the constant attacks on his character, he formed, with certain old friends, the so-called Black Tigers organisation and conducted a guerrilla campaign. He was frequently to be found hiding in bookshops, from where he would be carried off into detention. Each time, he escaped with the help of another generation. But, finally, he was cornered, and torn limb from limb.

Unconfirmed reports tell of cries of 'We're the finest tigers in the Jungle.' The spirit of Black Sambo lives on.

THE AUTHOR

Summer 1932

Kai Lung

We have just learnt that Kai Lung, the President of Chinese PEN, has died. He was widely known as the teller of stories which, though their author was humbly born, were written in what can only be described as a mandarin manner. They were exceptionally long-winded and always said in a hundred words what could more felicitously be said in ten.

Kai Lung kept in touch with his fellow members by wandering on foot throughout China, and was much admired for his stamina and his organising ability. Unfortunately, PEN was regarded as a subversive organisation in several Chinese states, and Kai Lung was often in conflict with the authorities. His normal method when on trial was to tell a continuing series of stories until, in order to stop the flow of his narrative, the presiding judge ordered his acquittal.

Last month, it was reported in Hong Kong, Kai Lung was again arrested, and on his appearance in court tried his usual method of defence. After a four-day hearing, the Mandarin Den Ning said that he had heard enough, and added 'Off with his head.' Kai Lung was still in mid-sentence when the sword fell.

While expressing his regrets, the Chairman of the Society of Authors, Mr Ernest Bramah Smith, said that it should be taken as a warning to all members of the Society that there are considerable dangers in long-windedness. He summed it up in the terse phrase: '*Vita longa, verba breva*'.

TOKYO TELEGRAPH

5th August 1945

GENERAL OKU KAMIMURA

Admiral Kazushige Hamagakuchi writes:

Our nation mourns the death reported yesterday of Oku Kamimura, General in our Imperial Army and famous son of a great warrior father.

His valour was a thing of legend, but he was also a most spiritual man, a man of profound thought and culture, who once said, 'I would sacrifice all my victories to have been the compiler of the leaves in the supreme poetical collection, the *Manyoshi.*'

As a Colonel in the war forced upon us by the Chinese in 1933, he distinguished himself by the rapid capture of the town of Jehol. He immediately put to death every inhabitant of that town, thereby bringing the blessings of peace and tranquillity to the entire province, and releasing many Imperial troops for similar defensive action elsewhere.

When, in 1943, the British forces were driven from Burma he was the general officer in charge of the administration and re-organisation of that country, which was filled with joy at its release by our Imperial Army from its brutal British yoke. But even before that — before the American warships had launched their attack on our gallant aircraft at Pearl Harbor — he had in his civilised wisdom and foresight drawn up a sacred code on the correct treatment of British and American prisoners-of-war. He explained how the necessary bind-

[*cont. on p. 90*]

ing and bayoneting of selected prisoners, to ensure a proper contrivance of noble calm and respect within the prisoners' generously furnished camps, must be regarded as a spiritual, long-extended religious rite, to be profoundly admired and greatly enjoyed.

Kamimura-san's vision and sagacity never faltered. We drank *sake* and spoke together only a few days before his death; he was calm and philosophical, bearing his years and his 23 stone lightly. At this moment when our nation's arms have suffered some small temporary setbacks (although most of the American fleet is sunk and the remainder is in full retreat), I repeat his great reassuring words:

> Our heroic nation cannot now lose this conflict. We have seized and liberated so many countries and territories and islands — for the Americans and British to attempt to retake them one by one in the face of our heroic resistance would take many years and cost them at least three millions in dead. The Americans and British will have no stomach for three million dead: at worst there will be a negotiated peace which will leave us masters of so much that our heroism has gained.
>
> There are, it is true, rumours that our vile enemies are perfecting some terrible weapon, a weapon so powerful that it could at one or two strokes destroy perhaps a quarter of a million people. We need have no fear of this.
>
> Had we such a weapon we would of course instantly use it, tramping through the ashes afterwards to bayonet the survivors, and so in one great coup bringing the supreme spiritual good, the triumph of Japanese arms. But, even if they should perfect such a weapon, the democracies do not have our spirit, courage and wisdom; and so they will never use it. They will fear what is called 'public opinion' — the pathetic bleatings of people throughout the world far from the noise of battle

[*cont. on p. 91*]

and the certainty of death. So they will never dare to employ it; they will lose a million or two lives vainly attempting to reach our sacred mainland, our *Shinkoku*, and then there will be peace; for us a glorious and victorious peace. We cannot lose this war.

General Oku Kamimura's calm, sure words may be his greatest memorial: 'We cannot lose this war.'

MANUSCRIPT CIRCULATED AMONG PERSIAN SHI'ITE AYATOLLAHS

AH **517** (*c.* 1124 AD)

OMAR KHAYYÁM
(Ghiyāthuddīn Abulfath Omar bin-Ibrāhīm, called 'al-Khayyāmī)

Lately, some 500 years after the foundation of our Faith at the Hejira, Omar Khayyám of Nishapur died at the Court of Mahmud of Ghuzni. He was there held in some esteem as a scholar, mathematician and astronomer — or, possibly, tent-maker.

This esteem was not deserved, and should be withheld. For he also wrote poetry and his quatrains, or *Rubaiyat*, reveal him rather as an undesirable person, deserving not of honour but of dismemberment. They display both Sufism and wantonness. Worse yet, they show a tolerant attitude to the evil of wine and strong drink. An especially notorious quatrain runs:

Here with a Loaf of Bread beneath the Bough,
A Flask of Wine, a Book of Verse — and Thou
Beside me singing in the Wilderness —
And Wilderness is Paradise enow.

Among other offensive couplets are:

The Grape that can with Logic absolute
The Two-and-Seventy jarring Sects confute . . .

[*cont. on p. 94*]

a tolerant attitude to the evil of wine and strong drink

and:

> I often wonder what the Vintners buy
> One half so precious as the Goods they sell.

Happily — for it would be an ill day if our enduring enemies, Judaism, Christianity and Buddhism, should learn of such weaknesses within our Faith — Omar Khayyám's wanton works will never find a translator and must soon fall into lasting obscurity.

THE TITIPU SUN

16th May 1885

Koko

In a sensational act of seppuku, Koko (34), the public executioner of this town, beheaded himself yesterday afternoon. One of his friends, Pish Tush, in an exclusive interview with the *Sun*, revealed that sexpot Koko had been much depressed after having been given the elbow by his intended bride, Lady Katisha (43), the ravishing member of the royal family.

The couple came together in remarkable circumstances when his intended, and her elected, partners eloped with each other. Koko's friends have been worried about his condition for some time. At least two earlier suicide attempts were frustrated by happy accidents. He was saved from drowning by the prompt action of a watcher on the river bank, Tit Willow (18), and in another fortunate escape he was prevented from drinking something with boiling oil in it.

It was revealed yesterday that in place of the customary suicide note, Koko left a little list.

From sources close to the palace it has been learnt that the office of Lord High Executioner has been taken over by Pooh-Bah in addition to his other duties. He is expected to start his operations tomorrow morning. The Mikado is said to be extremely satisfied.

The Lady Katisha was being comforted by friends and was unavailable to make a statement, but a friend said that it had all been a mistake. The elbow she had given him had been intended to be a love token. As her friend said: 'Here's a how-do-you-do.'

THE JUNGLIPORE BAZAAR AND RECORD

May 1935

D.E. Lawrence

Word is coming from England of the sad demise of that gallant soldier and writer of naughty stories, Mr D.E. Lawrence. It is given to few men in one short lifetime to have packed in so many jolly good experiences. Mr Lawrence was born in Nottingham, England, where his father was digging in the coal mines and doing many naughty things so that Mr Lawrence was born on the wrong side of the sheet, isn't it? He is digging up the past when the call of duty comes and he works among the dirty Arabs blowing up trains and things. He was also much loving camels. After the war he is writing a novel about his experiences with the camels but in order to escape from the dangers of libel actions he is changing the name of the beast and calling it *Kangaroo.* Later he is having trouble with the authorities and is prosecuted for writing *Seven Wisdom of Pillars,* of the lust of a mahout for a maharanee and a jolly good story it is. (Available from K. Lal bookshop at eight rupees.) He is also writing a very sexy book called *Women in Love* in collaboration with his wife, Miss Marie Spotes. The English *Kamasutra,* isn't it? It is the sad tidings that Mr Lawrence fell off his motorbicycle and died of the consumption. He is being much missed.

JERUSALEM TIMES

13th July 28 AD

Lazarus of Bethany

A Correction:
It is much regretted that in our issue of yesterday an obituary of Mr Lazarus appeared. This was due to a faulty report from a news agency. We are glad to state that, despite the fact that he was seriously ill, Mr Lazarus is now fully recovered. We offer our apologies to him and to his family, and much regret any inconvenience that the report of his premature demise may have caused.

POLICE REVIEW

November 1912

INSPECTOR A.N. LESTRADE

The death has been announced of one of Scotland Yard's most renowned crime investigators. He fully earned his nickname of 'Lestrade of the Yard' from the number of notable murder cases that he was able to solve.

The great investigator made his name in clearing up a perplexing South London murder which proved to have been connected with a feud among members of the Mormon sect. Later he was able to bring to justice the murderer of Lord St Simon and the fiend who slaughtered the Hon. Robert Adair.

Inspector Lestrade joined the force straight from school and served his probationary days on the beat in Whitechapel, where the knowledge he picked up of the Chinese community living there was invaluable to him in his later investigations. His promotion was rapid. He was always ready to admit that he owed much to the time that he spent as sergeant with another of the Yard's great figures, Mr Athelney Jones.

When Lestrade of the Yard was interviewed he always made it plain that his success was entirely due to routine police work. Flights of imagination or airy deductions, he insisted, had no place in police work.

One man to whom Inspector Lestrade was always ready to give credit was the police surgeon with whom he shared so many visits to the scenes of crime. This was Dr Watson, another thorough man, though the Inspec-

[*cont. on p. 99*]

tor deprecated the Doctor's habit of carrying a gun. 'Not a good example,' he is reported to have said. He was also not in favour of the Doctor's employment of wild young assistants. 'Of course,' he told an interviewer, 'a policeman needs a good nark. I had a fiddler once who told me a good thing or two, but he was never wholly reliable.'

After his long and successful period with the Murder Squad, Inspector Lestrade was transferred to the Drug Squad where he was instrumental in breaking a cocaine gang based in the premises of the Abbey National Building Society. The ring leader was sentenced to a long period of imprisonment. In mitigation it was pleaded that the fact that this man's brother, a senior civil servant, had defected, taking with him important Dreadnought plans, had caused him to take up a life of crime. Mr Justice Darling, sentencing this Sherlock Holmes, by trade a violinist, said that he agreed with Inspector Lestrade that this was a cock-and-bull story like most of the others that the cocaine user had concocted.

On his retirement Inspector Lestrade became the security officer at Madame Tussaud's, and he was well known in the Baker Street area where he had a commodious flat. After the death of his first wife, the Inspector married another Baker Street figure, his landlady Mrs Hudson. Their only son, Fabian, is also intended for a police career.

TRIPOLI TIMES

29th October 1986

THE EMPEROR MACASSAR

We learn with the deepest regret of the death in Monaco last week of the Emperor Macassar. He was 72, and it is only five years since he retired from his beneficent imperial rule of Upper Watta: although the previous imperialist colonialist British-Fascist regime had left Upper Watta an impoverished country, the Emperor was nevertheless enabled, through his wisdom, to secure his retirement with many millions of dollars in Swiss banks.

Since his dignified withdrawal, Upper Watta has fallen into grievous poverty. The despicable charities of the capitalist West have vainly tried to oil their consciences with petty contributions to help the nation's distress. The Emperor and his good friend, Field-Marshal Idi Amin — whose forward-looking rule of Uganda was no less cruelly terminated by evil Western plots — used sometimes to meet here in Tripoli and discuss with such sadness the endings of the good times for their countries.

The Emperor Macassar's government was indeed a model. He quickly abolished the absurd colonial inheritance of judges and courts, and attacked the problem of unemployment by increasing his Army tenfold. There were of course a few who resisted his strong, benign, centralised rule — CIA-financed dissidents calling themselves the Antimacassars — but they were quickly rounded up and shot or eaten.

[*cont. on p. 101*]

His essentially warm and democratic nature was testified by the overwhelming sadness displayed at his Monaco funeral by his last four wives, Miss Upper Watta 1978, Miss Upper Watta 1979, Miss Upper Watta 1980 and Miss Upper Watta 1981. Their bitter grief at the imperial passing must be shared by us all.

MY OBITUARY

1902

BY WILLIAM McGONAGALL
(Sir William Topaz McGonagall, Knight of the White Elephant of Burma)

To be sold for the benefit of my poor bereaved wife and family who will be much disturbed by my death.

This is the last poem that ever I shall write,
For I can see that my end is verily in sight.
It is a pity that I must die at this time,
Since it will leave the world without a man who can
  rhyme
In a way that will bring calm to the tossing waters of the
  Tay
And can sweep aside the rubbish of those critics who say
The world should heed the poor drivel of Eliot and
  Pound
Who have sma' inkling of how poetry should sound.

I am a man who has travelled far and wide. With that
  few men would quarrel.
Did I not on that great day in May almost see the Queen
  at Balmoral?
I stood my ground outside the great and good Victoria's
  gate
And would have seen her if that fell ghillie had not
  sealed my fate.
I did see the Czar, and Kaiser, too,
On a wet day when I was soaked through and through.

[*cont. on p. 104*]

'Did I not on that great day in May
almost see the Queen at Balmoral?'

Enough of that. My fate is sealed.
My grave is ready in that good Scottish earth at Potter's Field.
There is muckle little for my wife to inherit,
For the accursed Royal Literary Fund refused to grant my merit.
But those fools will cease their sneering when they know that after I cry finis,
My poems shall be recorded for the gramophone by that great actor-knight, Sir Alec Guinness.

HAMPSTEAD & HIGHGATE EXPRESS

2nd April 1883

Mr Charles Parkes

Mr Charles Parkes, who died on 14th March aged 64, was given a very fine funeral at Highgate Parish Church yesterday. Mr Parkes — although not from London, he has written a book on the capital — lodged with Mrs Esme Jelly of Bacon Lane, a well-known Hampstead resident who attended the funeral wearing a black bombazine dress, both elegant and appropriate to the sad occasion, and an unusual hat decorated with osprey and egret feathers. There were several other mourners, all tastefully dressed.

The music included the hymns 'Nearer My God to Thee' and 'My God and King', and there was also an anthem, 'O Praise the Great Lords' personally composed by the church's organist, Mr Foot, FRCO. The Vicar, The Reverend Bragg, despite his customary adenoidal trouble, conducted the beautiful service with his usual solemnity.

and an unusual hat decorated with osprey and egret feathers

HAMPSTEAD & HIGHGATE EXPRESS

3rd April 1883

We must apologise for some minor slips in the report in yesterday's paper — from our latest-joined reporter — of the funeral service in our Parish Church. The deceased's landlady's name is Mrs Jilly rather than Jelly (her late husband Mr Cooper Jilly was well known as a Heath Superintendent), and her dress had grey facings; the book written by the deceased was not entirely about London and was entitled *Das Kapital*, and his name, wrongly given as Mr Charles Parkes, was in fact Mr (Heinrich) Karl Marx.

CHILDREN'S NEWSPAPER

15th August 1928

Christopher Robin

Many young readers will be sad to learn of the sudden death of Christopher Robin, the central figure in four books written by his father, A.A. Milne. In a tragic accident he was found to have fallen downstairs. He was 6.

We have been asked to tell you that Christopher Robin is no relation of Mr C.R. Milne, the author and former bookseller, of Dartmouth, South Devon.

PIG BREEDER'S GAZETTE

October 1950

MR GEORGE ORWELL

Mr George Orwell, who died last month, was a very successful writer who got a lot of praise, particularly for his book *Animal Farm.* We cannot join in this praise, for he made his principal character, Napoleon, a pig, yet lacked true pig awareness.

Perhaps his was an over-refined background — he went from Eton to be an officer in the Indian Imperial Police — for he seems never really to have been on the pigs' wavelength, to have shared their problems, studied their psychology, known and loved them in pen and sty. Nor is it necessary to be a technical writer or veterinarian to achieve this: the writer of humorous novels, P.G. Wodehouse, profoundly understands the affections and motivations, as well as the requirements for accommodation and diet (protein for pig tissue building is essential) when writing about his noble pig, the Empress of Blandings.

Mr Orwell gives small consideration to the important factor of Pig Breeds. He describes Napoleon as 'an unusually large Berkshire boar': these are particularly fine pork pigs but probably not suited to political demagogy. And pig technologists generally feel that, when Mr Orwell has his pigs walking on two legs towards the end of his book, Landraces (those wonderful baconers) or even Essex Saddlebacks are breeds more likely to achieve this feat (it would involve transferring the animal's weight, at present borne on two

[*cont. on p. 110*]

toes, to all the four toes). He attributes no breed at all to his other leading pig personae; although Snowball might well be a Middle White, and Squealer seems to show the psychological traits of the Tamworth.

We understand that Mr Orwell wrote another book, called *1984*, which featured Rats. We hope he knew more of rats than pigs.

MORNING POST

1st July 1941

IGNACY JAN PADEREWSKI

The Hon. Charles Drax-Plunkett-Marjoribanks writes:

I read your yesterday's obituary to M. Paderewski with interest. I don't know much about him as a great pianist and composer, but I would like to add a memoir about him from the days about 1920 when he was Prime Minister of Poland.

I was Second Secretary in our Embassy in Warsaw; Odo (Bimbo) Fothergill-Spencer was First Secretary, and our chief was Sir Samson Courtenay, one of the most incisive minds in the diplomatic service. We were a very jolly mess and played a lot of auction bridge and 'Are You There, Moriarty?', a very funny game where a blindfold person on the floor tries to strike the questioner (also on the floor) with a rolled umbrella.

My official meetings with Paderewski were mostly about the Byelorussian question (the details of which I now forget), but he sometimes came informally to the Embassy, bringing with him Marshal Joe Pilsudski (the C-in-C who chased the Bolsheviki out of Poland), and very merry evenings we had. We played bridge, generally for groszy but sometimes for zlotys, and we taught Paderewski and Pilsudski to sing English folk songs like 'A Bicycle Made for Two' or 'Yes, We Have No Bananas'. Bimbo, who had a rapier wit, said they could form a music-hall duo called 'Like as Two Peas' (though in fact Pilsudski had an *enormous* moustache

[*cont. on p. 112*]

and Paderewski didn't), and we all roared with laughter.

Once or twice they brought young writers called Sloninski and Wierzynski and a queer young painter Tytus Czyewski (after a few drinks the irrepressible Bimbo cleverly said he was 'Tytus a Tick'). So I look back fondly to those happy Embassy evenings with Paderewski tinkling the ivories.

INVESTORS CHRONICLE

19th October 1936

MR PETER PAN

Word has been received from the Cayman Islands of the sudden death of one of the world's most brilliant and financial wizards, Peter Pan. Crocodile Enterprises and Tinkerbell Securities brought him immense wealth, and he was able to prove to a United Nations investigating committee that the charges against him of exploiting Indian labour were unfounded.

Pan's origins were obscure. It is thought that he had a Greek father and an Irish mother, and that 'Pan' was his anglicisation of his father's name. In his manner he appeared more English than the English, and was known to boast that he came from Kensington.

His earliest dealings in the Caribbean were mostly of an export and import sort, but he was soon into island property speculation on the never-never. His takeover battle with James Hook — the ex-Eton and Balliol financial genius, known for his raids on other smaller organisations as 'The Pirate King' — was one of the financial world's most celebrated and keenly fought campaigns. It was to end with Hook Incorporated being taken over by Crocodile Enterprises.

Although, for tax reasons, Pan was to live abroad for the greater part of the year, his London parties, held at the opulently furnished Tree House in his beloved adopted Kensington, were regarded as one of *the* great events of the London season. Each year a gala concert was given in the grounds of the Tree House on behalf of

[*cont. on p. 114*]

the charity which Pan founded, the Lost Boys.

When the finances of this charity came under investigation Pan was able to prove that he no longer had any connection with it and indeed that it was his former father-in-law, Mr Darling, who had been steadily milking the funds in order to keep up his kennel of greyhounds.

Pan was married to Wendy Darling at St James's Knightsbridge, in one of the weddings of the year. Eighteen months later, the marriage was annulled on the grounds of its non-consummation. In later years, Pan was normally to be seen at social occasions accompanied by his live-in companion, the beautiful raven-haired American usually known by the name she used as a model, Tiger Lily.

The winding up of Pan's estate is likely to prove one of the City's most complicated jobs. The outstanding firm of accountants, Smee, Starkey, has been engaged, it was learned from Pan's close business associate and probable successor at the head of the conglomerate, S. Soiled, a boyhood companion of Pan's. Asked by a reporter whether there were going to be many complications and whether it would prove a difficult task, Mr Soiled replied smilingly, 'Slightly.'

MANCHESTER GUARDIAN

28th February 1936

MR I.P. PAVLOV

Ivan Petrovitch Pavlov died in Leningrad on Friday. He was in his 88th year but had remained active and agile to the end.

Educated and trained in the old St Petersburg, Pavlov quickly became a well known prima ballerina within Russia. But world celebrity was only achieved (but then with a blazing suddenness) with the performances, with Nijinsky, in the Diaghilev Ballet in Paris in 1909.

The greatest triumph was to Saint-Saens' music in *Le Cygne*, in which the conditioned reflexes of live swans were astonishingly shown as associated with specific areas of brain cortex.

Pavlov, who was awarded the Nobel Prize for *Pas-de-Deux*, will enduringly be remembered as (in V. Dandre's moving words) 'a creature of transcendental grace and beauty, infinitely wise in the ways of the dance and the secretory nerves of the pancreas'.

MANCHESTER GUARDIAN

1st March 1936

We regret that in yesterday's issue of the *Manchester Guardian* the obituary of I.P. Pavlov, the distinguished Russian psychologist, inadvertently included material relating to Anna Pavlova, the Russian ballerina whose obituary we carried in 1931. This was due to some confusion in our composing room.

LA GACETA DEL GUARDIA CIVIL

18th July 1973

SEÑOR PABLO PICASSO

The average copper will be much saddened to learn of the death in the South of France of Pablo Picasso, an artist who will always be thought of as the policeman's friend. Before his great invention, the recording of mug-shots and the compilation of Identikit pictures had been a time-consuming business and the storage of the resulting likenesses was becoming increasingly difficult.

Don P.P., as the Police world called him, made a great breakthrough when he was in his late twenties by his skilful combination of the full face and the profile in a single picture. He developed this technique shortly after he went into plain clothes, having completed his uniformed service. Jokingly, he called this his 'Blue Period'. Then, the amount of 'bull' in the police got him down and he retired to the South of France where he spent the rest of his life. Unfortunately, his long researches into the possibility of producing a psycho-pattern for each individual as distinguishable as finger-prints was never completed.

THE SABBATH DAY

September 1617

FAKE RED INDIAN LOSES SCALP

By the *Sabbath Day* Insight Team (B. Jonson, T. Middleton, J. Webster, London; J.B. Poquelin, Paris; and J. Appleseed, The Colonies)

Intensive investigations over a period of months have now conclusively proved that the claims of the woman who called herself 'Pocahontas' and said that she was a Red Indian princess are entirely without foundation. In particular, her constant reiteration before large audiences that she had saved the life of a Captain John Smith by laying her head on top of his when a Red Indian executioner was about to kill him is utterly false.

We have now established that this woman's real name was Rebecca Rolfe and that she had always lived in Gravesend, Kent. Mrs Thora Kennedy (48) of Thamesview Road, Gravesend, remembers Rebecca as a girl: 'She was always a sunburnt little child — gypsy blood, I thought. Her passion was for dressing up.'

We have discovered a marriage certificate which names her as having married John Rolfe, a seaman. He cannot be contacted.

Searches through the Army and Navy Lists have produced no less than 26 Captain John Smiths, but 23 of them deny any knowledge of a 'Red Indian Maiden'. Of the other officers, one is said to be writing a learned book somewhere abroad and cannot be disturbed; one is at present in the Tower (for sedition), and the last one has never left Bootle. It is reasonable to assume that her

[*cont. on p. 119*]

Captain Smith does not exist.

Investigations in North America show that the method of execution used by the Powhatan Indians is not beheading. It is customary for the victim to be standing when he is clubbed to death. In addition, our reporter who interviewed Matoaka (62), chief of the Powhatan Indians, has established that the word 'Pocahontas' means 'Playful'. This surely is the key to the deception: Rebecca Rolfe was play-acting.

Repeated calls at Mrs Rolfe's last known address have been fruitless. Clearly this heartless woman has decamped.

STOP PRESS: The body of a woman was brought ashore at Dover last night from a ship bound for Virginia. It has been identified by the tattoo markings as that of Mrs Rebecca Rolfe (22), a Red Indian princess. Last week's investigations by the Insight Team were not entirely conclusive. Mrs Rebecca Rolfe, the Princess Pocahontas, was unfortunately confused with Mrs Rebecca Ralph of Gravesend. We would like to apologise for any inconvenience this might have caused. We have never made such an error before, and shall not do so again.

ANTI-SMOKING LEAGUE BROADSHEET

1st November 1618

Sir Walter Raleigh

Our beloved Sovereign, King James, last week struck a brave blow for our great cause with the Execution of Sir Walter Raleigh. Our noble Monarch has done more than prepare his sage treatise *Counterblast to Tobacco*; he has three days past executed that very villain, Sir Walter, who brought to these shores, from barbarous Virginia, the noxious and filthy habit of smoking.

It is known that Sir Walter was ever gullible, attending in his boyhood to the wild tales of old Devon mariners. He lacked wit and resource, yet rose to be Captain of the Guard at the Court of our late Majesty, Queen Elizabeth, through the regular monies paid to him by the Guild of Cloak and Pantaloon Makers, after the episode of the Royal Progress over a puddle which so invigorated the sales of cloaks throughout the Realm.

Yet he was touched with true wickedness when, returning from the lands of Indian and Carib with the hateful weed Tobacco, he instigated the odious Smoking of Pipes, to which our League and our great Monarch are opposed with such Resolution.

Sir Walter has done great harm to the health of this Nation, for apothecaries and chirurgeons of our persuasion give assurances that, before Smoking began, these Islands knew no rheum, phlegm or ague, nor complaints of heart, breast and lung. It can also send you blind.

Nor did Sir Walter and his adherents respect our

[*cont. on p. 122*]

the noxious and filthy habit of smoking

King and our Cause. Our banner at Tyburn, NO SMOKING, was rearranged by his rabble to NOSMO KING — and later a low player assumed this name for theatrical performances of the baser kind. Even at Execution — which Sir Walter bore calmly enough — the mob vouchsafed less of the spirit of holiday merriment which properly attends a beheading. Rather was it quiet, with a set of rogues freely smoking their pipes, led by a barefoot Yorkshire crop-ear, one Wilson, who loudly declared that 'The pouch in your pocket still hath its full worth.'

Foolhardy words. For, to our League's great gladness, with Sir Walter the Arch-Smoker, dead, this Evil cannot now endure more than a few quarters yet.

MORNING POST

15th May 1926

KINGSLEY ROCKALL

Our Assistant Sporting Correspondent writes:

I write with deep emotion of the death today of my colleague, Kingsley Rockall, for 30 years the Sporting Correspondent of this newspaper. It has been my high privilege to have been his assistant for the past decade.

When he wrote of Cricket, you could smell the fresh-mown grass of the outfield; when he wrote of Football, you could sense the deeper feelings of the huge, well-ordered crowds; when he wrote of Racing, the brilliance of the jockeys' silks gleamed and flashed before your eyes.

Kingsley's life was sport. Since his wife's death he lived at his Club, the Combined Sportsman, and much of every summer was spent at Lord's where Test Matches and Gentleman *v* Players were his chief delight. How often has he said to me, 'Tiffin, Tiffin old friend, I'll do the actual reporting while you get the flavour of the crowd in the Tavern.'

As I stood today, looking down at his kind, sweet, well-remembered face, stilled in death, and realised I would never again hear his deep friendly voice, everything became a blur to me; his familiar features, the many gathered grieving relations and friends, all vanished from my sight in an overwhelming haze of deep and sad emotion.

I and our countless readers must be at one in our profound grief at Kingsley's passing.

MORNING POST

17th May 1926

We regret that our readers were misinformed about our Sporting Correspondent, Kingsley Rockall, in our issue of 15th May. The item was written by Tiffin O'Lush who was, until yesterday, Assistant Sporting Correspondent: Mr O'Lush apparently misunderstood the nature of his assignment, which was not to a death but to a marriage.

Kingsley Rockall is in fact in excellent health and will return to these columns on Monday week from his honeymoon at Frinton-on-Sea.

THE STRATFORD-UPON-AVON ADVERTISER

25th April 1616

MR WILLIAM SHAKESPEARE

The death has been announced of the local property developer, Mr William Shakespeare (53), who will be best known in this area as the son of a former Mayor of Stratford, Mr John Shakespeare, a man much respected in the community. He will also, of course, be remembered for having won the hand of that celebrated local beauty queen, Miss Anne Hathaway (Miss Shottery, 1581). Young Mr Shakespeare, who made his home at New Place during the last few years, was quite a lad in his day. Old Stratfordians remember stories of the young man and his roistering companions chasing the deer in Charlecote Park, and some think that he was very lucky to escape execution. Mr Shakespeare attended Stratford Grammar School where he was remembered as a good student, though he had some difficulty with Latin and it was decided that he should not attempt Greek.

After leaving school Mr Shakespeare became a teacher and left the town. He had obviously done well, for he returned after successful property speculation in London to start business here. He was a well-known figure at the Swan Tavern where he used to drop hints that he had literary connections, though in less convivial moments he would admit that this consisted of acting as speechwriter for Sir Francis Bacon. Mr Shakespeare also claimed to be something of a poet, but this is unlikely. The only poem of his that has so far been

[*cont. on p. 126*]

published is an epitaph which he said he would like placed on his tomb. This is just doggerel and his ear is not very good for rhymes. He is survived by his widow and one of his twin children, Judith. Let us say to him that jocular farewell that he used to address to his mates at the Swan: 'Goodnight, Sweet Prince.' Obviously, a quotation from something. He never said what.

THE TIMES

10th June 1831

Mrs Sarah Siddons

Sarah Siddons is dead. She was 76 years of age but to the nation's theatre-lovers it seems but yesterday that, on the magical evening of 9th June 1818, she made her final and unforgettable appearance at Covent Garden.

When she was born in Brecon, she was born to acting, with Roger Kemble her father, John Philip Kemble her brother. At 20 she was playing with Mr Garrick's company at Drury Lane. Her triumphs thereafter were too numerous to recapitulate: they included most notably Euphrasia, Belvedira, Calista and Jane Shore and — from her memorable Shakespearian range — Desdemona, Volumnia and Lady Macbeth. So powerfully did her great Shakespearian roles affect her that she was sometimes found to assume the Bard's language in ordinary speech, and ask in pentameters that the pepper be passed.

This leads us to advert to Mrs Siddons' dignity and nobility, not only upon the stage but in the manner of her unblemished private life.

It would be idle to deny that before Mrs Siddons most actresses were little better than courtesans. The scurrilous gossip of the *Morning Post* at the end of the last century (before Mr Stuart bought it), gossip so coarse and gross that the *Post*'s Editor, Henry Bate, was rightly jailed for it, was nonetheless near to truth when it dealt of actresses. And if not wanton and silly, then they were doubly silly. They became tiresomely

[*cont. on p. 128*]

concerned with 'movements' or 'causes', making much pretty noise about them without much understanding what they were about. And they were in a state of constant worry concerning their beauty, prattling endlessly about perfumed powders of French chalk and orris root or scented pomades of beeswax and lard; even making advertisements for these trivial preparations.

As she has changed our notions of acting, so has Mrs Siddons changed the notion of what an actress need be. If in future ages a newspaper should publish columns of malice and gossip such as those in the old *Morning Post* (unlikely, since no educated person would wish to read them) then they should no longer have occasion to feature the lives and amours of actresses, the devices by which they strive to retain their beauty, their excited enthusiasms for tedious 'causes'.

Posterity may find that one of Mrs Siddons' most inestimable services to the stage was to establish for future actresses that they need be neither whores nor bores.

PLAIN ENGLISH

December 1930

CANON W.A. SPOONER

It is with the reepest degret that we announce the detimely unwise of Canon William Spooner, the Warden of Queue Knowledge, an acknowledged paster of mose and conversationalist of note.

His height wear and ink pies proclaimed that he was almost an albino. His seekly wermons in the Challage Copel appealed to fro and fend alike. They fat at his seat and weeded his herds before woeing on their gay. Spain Pleach was his wife's lurk. We pawn his massing.

They fat at his seat and weeded his herds

THE DUNTHEBOYZAN

Trinity Term, 1845

The Headmaster, Wackford Squeers

An Old Boy writes:

Only my presence in Botany Bay has prevented me writing earlier to express my extreme regret at the passing of one of the great headmasters of our time. Wackford Squeers ('Old Wackers', as we used affectionately to call him) will long be remembered by all his Old Boys for his practical approach to education. I can attest that since my arrival in this country I have been able to put into practice many of the skills that he taught us so thoroughly. I now have one of the most substantial window-cleaning businesses in Sydney, and I owe this all to old 'Wackers'. 'Winders' (he affected the old spelling, and who shall argue with him), he wrote on the board, and made sure by practical teaching that not a corner of any of the school panes was left with a smear in it.

As one of the more enlightened headmasters, he did not bother to burden young minds with the knowledge of dead languages, preferring to prepare his charges for the School of Life. We left Dotheboys Hall sound in body and mind. I am sure that I am not alone in ascribing my regularity to the healthy regime set up and administered by good old Mrs Squeers. I can assure you that my children enjoy the fine old taste of brimstone and treacle as much as I did. Those of us who were in the senior forms at the time were greatly upset

[*cont. on p. 132*]

when Mr Squeers announced to us one morning that he was finding it necessary to retire. I must say that I have always blamed this unhappy event (disastrous for the smooth running of the school) on the arrival of that young assistant master from one of those trendy left-wing teachers' training colleges. I cannot remember his name, but I do recall we nicknamed him 'Nickle-bottom'. When I heard that he had run off with that weed Smike and that they had both gone on the stage I was not a bit surprised. The reforms that he tried to institute were not at all in the spirit that made Dotheboys Hall a great school. My deepest condolences to Mrs and Miss Squeers. My enforced stay in these parts in quarters that seem like the old alma mater has enabled me to gain a place on the local school board, and I am glad to say that we are setting up a number of establishments which will perpetuate the proud name of Wackford Squeers. You may be interested to know that the local word (it comes from the abo) for 'squeers' is 'Geelong'. Old Wackers has his memorial here, with our proud cry: 'Good on yer, School.'

THE BETHLEHEM VILLAGE ECHO

31st December 35

Saint Stephen

He was *stoned.*

PLAID CYMRU BULLETIN

25th November 1953

Mr Dylan Thomas

Too much has been written about Dylan Thomas who has died in the USA, at the early age of 39, apparently from drink. He was constantly called a Welsh poet which of course he wasn't since all his alleged poems were written in a foreign tongue — English. Only once did he use — indeed invent — a really beautiful Welsh word, and that was when he gave the village in *Under Milk Wood* the exquisite name of Llareggub. In that word is much of the history, mystery and romance of our supreme Celtic heritage, which he otherwise ignored.

One of our devoted members Dai Fawkes had planned to blow up Dylan's house in Laugharne, and therefore asked him in the bar in Browns Hotel what was his address. Dai had difficulties with blocks of wax and syringing of his ears, and did not properly hear the reply, 'The Boat House'. There was some trouble when he later blew up Farmer Wynford Thomas's goat house as the farmer had to live on goat stew for weeks and cancelled his subscription to our cause. Otherwise we would, in a civilised way, have shown the so-called Welsh poet just what the real Welsh thought of him.

had to live on goat stew for weeks

THE UK PRESS GAZETTE

18th October 1856

Sweeney Todd

Many Fleetstreeters will be much shocked by the unexpected death of that popular character with the foaming brush, Sweeney Todd, widely known for his prowess with the scissors and comb as 'the Demon'. No one gave a shorter back and sides or left a cleaner chin. A French sailor in El Vino was heard to remark that he had never had a closer shave. Older hands will know that it was the custom of the Street for someone on picking up his redundancy cheque to go for one last treatment at the hands of Old Sweeney. He saw them off in great style. His premises have been taken over by a Mr Murdoch. Welcome to the Street, Rupert.

Mrs Lovett's popular pie shop, at 135 Fleet Street, well-known for the meatiness of its pies and the pleasantness of the manner in which they were served, has closed down. It is understood that the new management will concentrate on soul food.

THE TIMES

14th April 1973

LIEUTENANT-COLONEL THE VISCOUNT TURBINGER

Lieutenant-Colonel Lord Turbinger died on Tuesday night in his sleep at his family home near Charlbury. He was 74.

Sebastian Oliver Daniel Turbinger was the eldest son of the fourth Viscount. Educated at Wellington and Woolwich, he was commissioned into the Royal Artillery a few days after the 1918 Armistice. He was — save for a short posting as a military attaché — a regimental soldier for his entire career: to his regret he was regarded in the 1939-45 war as essentially a trainer of men, and commanded the 302nd Field Regt RA stationed in Cannock throughout the hostilities.

On his father's death in 1947 Colonel Turbinger succeeded to the title, and retired from the Army. He was Deputy Lieutenant of Oxfordshire 1958-60; served on the General Synod of the Church Assembly, and was for 25 years Chairman of the Bench of Chipping Stoat.

He married, in 1934, Edythe, daughter of the Bishop of Bath and Wells. His two sons both entered the church: the elder, Sebastian Temple Lang, who succeeds him, is at present Vicar of St Grummett's, Woodstock.

although he had a fine strong voice, was tone deaf and totally unmusical

THE TIMES

17th April 1973

C O'H D V L de L-R writes:

I read with sadness your obituary of my old friend Sebastian Turbinger, which nevertheless revived happy memories of our times together at the British Embassy in Budapest when he was military attaché there in the late 1920s.

Old Turbot or Fishface, as we invariably called him, was the life and soul of Budapest nightlife. He was on close terms — always insisting that it was essential to his duties — with every chorus girl in the eleven main nightclubs in the city's Belvaros quarter. My favourite recollection of Sebastian is on Hallowe'en night when, standing naked on the Andrassy Statue, he played a gypsy violin to a large crowd. Sebastian, although he had a fine strong voice, was tone deaf and totally unmusical. The violinist was compensated for the destruction of his instrument when he came out of hospital some weeks later: he took it all very sportingly as a tremendous lark.

Later, however, both Sebastian and Admiral Horthy, the Regent of Hungary, fell in love with Espadrille, an exotic tassel dancer at his favourite night spot, L'Aphrodisiac. Although now suffering from a painful disease as a consequence of his work, Sebastian determined to challenge the Regent to a duel, and arranged for the first Viscount's set of duelling pistols to be sent from Charlbury. When our Ambassador learned, with regret, that the Admiral was a very poor shot, however, he decreed that 'Fishface must go back to gunnery', and the Embassy lost its liveliest member.

THE CAMBRIDGE DAIRY NEWS

Summer 1951

Ludwig Wittgenstein

All the lads at the Cambridge depot of Rapid Dairies will be sad to hear of the early death of one of their most popular former colleagues, Ludwig Wittgenstein. 'Witty' as he was so aptly nicknamed by the other milkies, was always the centre of the group which gathered round the piano after the daily rounds were done. His fund of stories was much appreciated, though it was a good thing that no ladies were present. It is a great tribute to the sunniness of his disposition that someone who had the misfortune to be born outside this country should have fitted in so well. When he handed in his notice to go and work for one of the colleges in some capacity or other, all the boys at the depot gave him their traditional send-off, smashing the pintas round his feet. And as he left, the wise words of the manager were ringing in his ears: 'Think logical. Think positive.' We hope he did.

FUNDAMENTALIST NEWS

6th June 1912

MR WILBUR WRIGHT

We of course regret the death last week, at the age of 45, of Mr Wilbur Wright. But, whilst admiring the courage — indeed, foolhardiness — of Wilbur Wright and his brother, Orville, in their experiments with heavier-than-air machines, we can only deeply deplore the modest success they have achieved.

The craze cannot continue. If God had intended man to fly, He would have given him wings. But He did not, and the idea of flying must fail. The pity is that the Wright brothers did not pursue their original avocation as manufacturers of bicycles, which gave opportunities for healthful exercise and can lead to increased chapel attendances.